LEARNING TO LEAD COMPUTING
A guide for teachers & leaders

Karl McGrath
& Allen Tsui

Although every effort has been made to ensure that website addresses are correct at time of going to press, Hachette Learning cannot be held responsible for the content of any website mentioned in this book. It is sometimes possible to find a relocated web page by typing in the address of the home page for a website in the URL window of your browser.

Hachette UK's policy is to use papers that are natural, renewable and recyclable products and made from wood grown in well-managed forests and other controlled sources. The logging and manufacturing processes are expected to conform to the environmental regulations of the country of origin.

To order, please visit www.HachetteLearning.com or contact Customer Service at education@hachette.co.uk / +44 (0)1235 827827.

ISBN: 978 1 915261939

© Karl McGrath and Allen Tsui 2025

First published in 2025 by
Hachette Learning,
An Hachette UK Company
Carmelite House
50 Victoria Embankment
London EC4Y 0DZ
www.HachetteLearning.com

The authorised representative in the EEA is Hachette Ireland, 8 Castlecourt Centre, Dublin 15, D15 XTP3, Ireland (email: info@hbgi.ie)

Impression number   10 9 8 7 6 5 4 3 2 1
Year   2029 2028 2027 2026 2025

All rights reserved. Apart from any use permitted under UK copyright law, no part of this publication may be reproduced or transmitted in any form or by any means, electronic or mechanical, including photocopying and recording, or held within any information storage and retrieval system, without permission in writing from the publisher or under licence from the Copyright Licensing Agency Limited. Further details of such licences (for reprographic reproduction) may be obtained from the Copyright Licensing Agency Limited, www.cla.co.uk

Cover photo

Illustrations by DC Graphic Design Limited, Hextable, Kent.

Typeset in the UK.

Printed in the UK.

A catalogue record for this title is available from the British Library.

Together we unlock every learner's unique potential

At Hachette Learning (formerly Hodder Education), there's one thing we're certain about. No two students learn the same way. That's why our approach to teaching begins by recognising the needs of individuals first.

Our mission is to allow every learner to fulfil their unique potential by empowering those who teach them. From our expert teaching and learning resources to our digital educational tools that make learning easier and more accessible for all, we provide solutions designed to maximise the impact of learning for every teacher, parent and student.

Aligned to our parent company, Hachette Livre, founded in 1826, we pride ourselves on being a learning solutions provider with a global footprint.

www.hachettelearning.com

Karl McGrath began working in schools as a volunteer in a primary classroom. He soon became a Learning & Equalities Mentor, creating films and animations to help children access the curriculum in innovative ways. This sparked his passion for computing and its role in education. While still a Newly Qualified Teacher (NQT), Karl became the computing lead at his school. Here, he embraced his interest in computing and was successful in becoming a Barefoot Ambassador, a CAS community leader, and an NCCE facilitator. Currently, as the curriculum task design lead and computing lead at Benton Park Primary School, Karl ensures the curriculum aligns with student tasks with a particular focus on empowering subject leads to find and nurture their subject integrity. Karl is a passionate advocate for 'concept before code' and ensuring children are empowered to become confident 'digital creators' as opposed to passive digital users. He continues to share his expertise and wisdom through CPD sessions and now, along with Allen, this book.

Allen Tsui has been subject lead for computing at a primary school in East London since September 2020. As the primary Allen works for is part of a multi academy Trust which includes secondary schools, Allen has been tasked with working and supporting the secondaries with preparing their GCSE and A-level students for their computer science examinations. Allen is a passionate advocate for physical computing products and online learning platforms, as well as building connections with teachers to support their professional development.

ACKNOWLEDGMENTS

This book would not have been possible without the help and support of so many people.

Firstly, our heartfelt thanks to John Catt for believing in this project and agreeing to publish our work. Your unwavering encouragement and support throughout this process has been invaluable. A special thank you to our editor, Anthony Green, whose expertise and guidance brought this book to life.

We are profoundly grateful to Mary Myatt and Miles Berry for their thoughtful reflections and insights on this book. Their combined experience is incredibly valued and has enriched this work.

Karl:

To my wife, Claire – your inspiration, encouragement and patience have been the foundation of my career and this book. Thank you for standing by me, especially during late nights spent writing. Your unwavering support means everything.

To my children, Nora and Wilf – thank you for reminding me of the joy and wonder of learning every day. Your curiosity inspires me beyond measure, and I am so proud to be your dad.

I also extend my thanks to my colleagues at West Jesmond Primary and Benton Park Primary School. Your dedication to education and openness to innovation have shaped my understanding of purposeful subject leadership. Thank you for embracing new ideas in computing education – and for your patience as I enthusiastically shared my passion for unplugged computing!

Finally, to my collaborators at the National Centre for Computing Education (NCCE) and Computing at School (CAS) – your shared vision, insights and expertise have been transformative. Your influence is woven into every page of this book, and this achievement is as much yours as it is mine.

To every educator I've learned from, listened to, and borrowed time from – you are the metaphorical software enhancements that have allowed me to grow as a teacher and leader.

Allen:

My biggest thanks has to go to Karl McGrath for inviting me to be his co-author. Through my experiences of working with secondary school-aged students since 2020, I've realized the pedagogical principles are not that different. Secondaries benefit from the focus or structure of public examination expectations and ensuring children want to continue studying computing beyond the age of 14. Thanks as well for the love, support and tolerance of so many. They know who they are.

CONTENTS

Acknowledgments _____v

Forewords _____ viii

Chapter 1 Introduction: Don't panic! _____1

Chapter 2 Who do we think we are? _____9

Chapter 3 What is computing? _____15

Chapter 4 Where do I start? Purpose _____37

Chapter 5 What next? Implementation _____53

Chapter 6 How do I know? Assessment _____63

Chapter 7 Where can I learn more? _____69

Chapter 8 What is emerging? _____73

References _____77

FOREWORDS

The great strides made in curriculum discussion and development in the past few years have re-energised conversations about what needs to be taught and how best to do so. The curriculum project is never-ending. This is not to consider it as a chore, but rather as an interesting, ongoing strand of professional endeavour which, if done well, and with sufficient time attached to it, is intellectually rewarding.

It's the idea that the work is never finished and that we should decide to embrace its ongoing nature that led John Tomsett and I to refer to the curriculum series as 'Huh', because 'Huh' is the Egyptian god of creativity, renewal and everlasting things.

Learning to Lead Computing absolutely captures the spirit of curriculum development being iterative and intellectually satisfying. In Karl McGrath and Allen Tsui, we have two remarkable advocates for the subject. They are unapologetically ambitious for young people's entitlement to a powerful computing curriculum.

It's wonderful to see the rigour and vigour with which they approach their work. And they are so enthusiastic that as you read this book, you will be caught up in their enthusiasm too! Take this as an example:

> *'However we would like to advocate for a shift in how you approach computing leadership and subject development. Let's repeat that statement from the National Curriculum: "Computational thinking and creativity to understand and change the world." That's the heart of what you're building.'*
>
> **McGrath and Tsui, 2025, p.16**

The way that Karl and Allen exhort us to treat the subject with respect without becoming intimidated by its gigantic space and potential is very, very clever. As you take in their arguments you will feel both excited and encouraged. This is no mean feat, but the two have managed to communicate in a way that is both aspirational and approachable. It's a winning combination and it's rare.

Each subject we teach our young people has bespoke principles, concepts and ways of working. These elements in computing are demanding and might be daunting. However, the genius of these two is that they break them down with analogies and explanations, so that you will find yourself thinking 'Ah that's how it works!' and 'How interesting!' It's like having two wise and friendly cousins guiding you through and showing you all the exciting potential for the subject.

I predict *Learning to Lead Computing* will be read and enjoyed by many professionals beyond the subject itself. It's a masterclass in capturing and communicating the essence and practicalities of teaching. As the authors say: 'Computer science is complex, but it needn't be' and this book absolutely lives up to that.

Mary Myatt

Education writer and speaker

11 January 2025

There are parallels between the world of software engineering and that of subject leadership in schools. Once upon a time, a 'waterfall' approach might have worked: policymakers provide a list of requirements – the national curriculum programmes of study; the subject leaders uses this to design a scheme of work or long-term plan; their colleagues set about teaching this to their pupils; assessment data allows the subject leader to evaluate the effectiveness of the planning and its' teaching; and then adjustments are made. Whilst this *can* still work in software engineering, and even teaching, we know that a more agile approach is likely to be more effective.

We've come to recognise that processes and tools, documentation and planning do matter, but they're not the only things that matter, and might not be the most important things. Subject leadership is much more about the individuals involved, and the leaders' interactions with them; it's about the effectiveness of computing education in the school or trust; it's about a collegial approach which recognises, values and develops the expertise of all involved; and it has to be about responding to change.

In computing, and computing education, the pace of change seems to be ever increasing. The subject at school level seems so much closer to the cutting edge of the discipline itself than many other school subjects. For school computing to remain relevant and engaging, those leading it need to think through the impact of technological and societal change, ensuring their colleagues are equipped to teach, and thus their pupils learn, about emerging areas like generative AI, quantum computing and the risks of screen time and social media.

Karl and Allen have done much to advance computing in schools through their communities and networks. In this book, they share generously their expertise and experience in teaching and leading computing, offering practical advice and, whilst their focus is on the leadership of computing, the advice they offer will resonate with teachers and those leading other subjects too.

Miles Berry

University of Roehampton

March 2025

CHAPTER 1
INTRODUCTION: DON'T PANIC!

Computing is broad. Like, really broad. You won't believe how truly, vastly broad it really is!

Joking aside, it's true. Computing is a subject that the Department for Education (DfE) reduced into a programme of study with just 25 bullet points (2013). This document, easily printed on five A4 pages, covers 11 years of teaching. Yet, computing can stretch its arms out and touch, in some form or another, every subject across the national curriculum. Moreover, the nuances of the subject are tangentially connected to our lives, and to the lives of the children in our care.

However, DON'T PANIC! We are your guides through the vast galaxy that is computing.

Some of you might have requested or taken an active interest in becoming the subject lead for computing, which is great. More commonly, though, particularly in primary schools, and increasingly in secondary schools due to the recruitment crisis of subject specialists, subject leadership roles might have been thrust upon you. It's not the worst thing to happen. Then there are those of you already leading maths or science, barely holding things together, only to have computing slipped under the metaphorical door as well. None of this is fair. Our system of subject leadership can be a minefield, and without the right experience or CPD, computing can quickly confuse and swamp you.

The reality is that many schools are financially stretched and time-poor. Even those schools lucky enough to have economies of scale and a leadership structure that enables the development of specialists face their own challenges. Our hope is that our combined experience will help you to avoid the trip hazards and logjams we have already navigated in our careers.

In a system where more subject leads are expected to develop a subject in which they either have a base knowledge or little interest, it's incredibly important to have a network or support system. In this book, we aim to be your support. Some of you will read it cover to cover, diligently taking notes, while others will dip in as needed. Consider us your guide through the vast galaxy that is computing leadership – a subject we believe to be uniquely specialist and incredibly enjoyable to lead.

You will no doubt feel our passion for computing dripping from every paragraph. We love computing. We are both advocates for it as a subject, and despite the tectonic shifts in the digital landscape since it emerged in the national curriculum, it is more relevant now than ever before.

Back in 2013, the iPad was only three years old and Minecraft was the biggest online game in the world. It seemed a simpler time. Snapchat dominated young users' social media, and Twitter had just launched Vine. But the landscape has changed since then.

Today, children consume information from morning to night, and their playgrounds are now FaceTime, TikTok and Fortnite. Politicians and stakeholders like to trumpet that computing is key to developing digital literacy and critical thinking. We disagree. A well-rounded, knowledge-rich curriculum with well-thought-out subject disciplines is integral to developing critical thinkers.

Computing is an incredibly important component of this. While some may argue that subjects such as French or computing should be relegated to Year 7, we would disagree. Computing is about empowering children to become confident digital creators. These children are on the edge of a digital world we can't yet fully imagine: as these so-called 'digital natives' survey (or even embark on) the digital landscape like a video game character heading out on a daring quest, and it's our job to equip them, although thankfully, our children's journey is much less frightful.

We've been lucky. We've had support from our schools and leaders to attend CPD, though occasionally that support had to be secured by stealth (but that's another story!). Our collaboration began during a time of global turmoil, the Covid-19 pandemic in 2020. Out of that upheaval came opportunities to transform the learning landscape. Buoyed by our workplace's support, we felt confident to take on this immense task.

There's plenty of excellent CPD available, but we know it's not always easy to attend. So, we hope this book will show you the incredible versatility of computing, without overwhelming you. We believe you'll see how computing can be a tool for children to express themselves confidently, creatively and safely as change-making, future-shaping digital citizens. You will be able to support them to be resilient and responsive to the ever-evolving online world. And, we hope this book empowers you to lead a subject and build a curriculum you can be proud of.

Computing is broad, but it's versatile, exciting and incredibly enriching. So, although it can be challenging, we hope you enjoy it.

Now that we can take a deep breath together, the first thing you need to do is...WAIT! Don't do anything yet. Just sit with the fact that you're now the computing lead. You might feel the urge to prove yourself, or be frantically searching online for 'computing curriculum', 'algorithms' and 'Scratch', trying to absorb everything at once. Or, maybe you've studied computer science at university, or this might be your second time as computing lead. Even so, wait. Take time to understand the role, the subject and the context.

Do nothing, you say?

Yes, we know it sounds counterintuitive, but trust us. We're speaking from experience. We've been eager to prove ourselves too. But if we could do it all again, we'd slow down. We would choose slow progress over rapid progress any day.

Karl: I was desperate to have computing as a responsibility. At this point for me, I didn't really have the opportunity to think about what I wanted to do. To start with, I was given a third of the computing curriculum. I happily took it, as I wanted to show I could offer something else to the school. I was tasked with developing the computer science strand of our schools computing curriculum. However, I didn't stop or breathe. I launched into a staff survey, testing out apps and looking at what I could spend on tech in the first year. The answer? Nothing.

Allen: I'll be honest. I've been sitting on the sidelines where computing is concerned, as I'm one of those subject leads who wanted the role ever since I first stepped foot into a classroom back in 2010. I'm fortunate enough, since 2020, to have been associated with a family of schools who have different needs where computing is concerned. There are colleagues who are supremely enthusiastic about what they want to teach and how. There are others who are grateful for the support that the wider computing teaching community can provide.

Our advice to you is clear: take a deep breath and wait. But for how long? We can understand your concern. Below are some questions that might prove helpful. We would suggest you try to answer these with the first thing that comes to your mind, because you might be an ECT, or feel that you have no idea about the type of computing teaching at your school. We guarantee though that you will have a greater insight than you imagine.

Take time to reflect on these questions. Your answers might surprise you, and they will be instrumental in enabling you to start to plan your next steps.

- What does computing look like in your class?
- What does computing look like in your school?
- What would/do the children in your class say about computing?
- If you could sum up computing in three words, what would they be?

Your first instinct might be to spend your time excitedly looking for hardware, the next hot app or training opportunities. DON'T. Take a step back and wait. Think about your answers to these questions. It may sound clichéd, but what is your 'why'? Other than 'because the national curriculum tells me so', why is computing taught at your school? Why do you value computing as a subject? Or do you? These are additional questions to consider.

In writing this book, we have made the bold assumption that you requested the position of computing lead, or that you accepted gleefully. However, this might not have been the case. We imagine that a few scenarios played out before and after you said 'yes' to accepting the role, assuming you didn't need convincing to lead computing in your school. Now that you hold the coveted position, some of these scenarios might have crossed your mind:

- Your headteacher/deputy or other senior leader will have given you a list of actions to 'sort'. From a secondary school standpoint, the issue will be whether computing at key stage 3 supports learning across the rest of the curriculum, and ensuring that enough interest is generated for learning the subject at key stage 4 and beyond.
- Through comments or observations of other teachers, you might already have noticed an area of need within the school (this can often be a good place to start thinking about your plans).
- Your previous computing lead has done a clear and detailed handover. This might seem intimidating but really, have the confidence in yourself to be the subject lead that you want to be. The technological landscape is always evolving, and periodically reviewing the content for teaching computing is worthwhile.

Becoming a quiet detective

Putting your thoughts into practice can be tricky. Your answers and the thinking behind them are a good place to start. Now become a quiet detective: explore what resources already exist, if anything. If nothing exists, why? Is there a reason? Is it financial or other? An empty box is still a box; the absence of something tells you a lot. If equipment or resources do exist, should they? If you are taking over for someone, you are likely to be approached with tips or advice from others. It is important here to be mindful of the fact that you could be taking over from someone who might not have wanted to lose the lead computing role, or is expecting to regain it. This might be after parental leave or a short-term role change.

Good sleuths leave no stone unturned, which is incredibly important because you will probably find a wealth of planning, resources or kit that has been buried – either in the digital graveyard, or in 'that' cupboard in school, a well-known hiding spot for all manner of education equipment. What you do with it is another matter.

When (or if) you find any morsels of resources, you should use this as a basis for further investigation. It would be useful to approach an experienced member of staff and ask:

- How old is this piece of equipment/resource?
- Have they used it or seen it before?
- Do they know what you're talking about?

If the equipment was generated/made before 2014, it is not likely to be immediately useful. However, resources can often be tweaked or adapted to suit a newer purpose or audience. Take, for example, The Valiant Roamer® (https://valiant-technology.com/uk/docs/Roamer_Activity_Book.pdf).

The Valiant Roamer® was an educational robot, a development of the Turtle-type robots invented originally, in the late 1960s, by MIT's Seymour Papert. The Turtle was part of LOGO – a computer language designed for very young children – but it was capable of challenging and developing the intellect of much older pupils. Students used LOGO to program solutions to problems, particularly mathematical problems. Now the Roamer itself has long since retired, although we would love to hear about any that remain in schools today. However, Figure 1.1 shows how Karl adapted the 'Demolition' Roamer for his own use. Using the resource booklet as an idea to develop problems and tasks for the BeeBot or 'FakeBot' is a perfect way to utilise older equipment and resources.

Demolition BeeBot

Build a tower from empty boxes or polystyrene blocks.

Position the 🐝 at any starting point.

Instruct the 🐝 to knock down the tower, using moves and turns.

Obstacles may be placed in the path which the 🐝 must avoid during demolition.

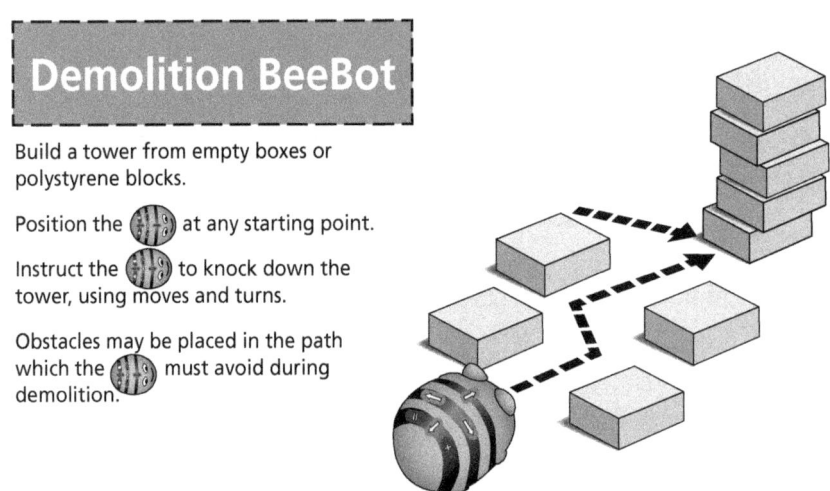

▲ Figure 1.1 The Demolition Beebot

Roundtables and teacher research groups

Considering setting up a small group of trusted advisers. We're not suggesting selecting a group of your trusted 'besties', but rather a group of confident teachers that you know will be honest and are happy to try new things. This teacher research group (TRG) could be a sounding board for any ideas or suggestions, particularly when you're thinking about what to implement. They will also be your test group, if you need to test something on just one or two teachers instead of the entire staff. We liken this to lighting 'little fires', metaphorically of course. School development and improvement can be difficult, which is why it's important not to overwhelm others. Within your TRG you can suggest strategies, resources and trials, and this should provide a productive space to ensure that whatever you intend to roll out to the wider teacher base is useful.

Being a subject lead for computing can also be a lonely role, as you might be the only advocate for the subject in the school. You might already be wearing many leadership hats, and computing is the beading on the brim. So, make use of the support available on social media networks, as it is the greatest and biggest virtual staffroom.

If you see blank faces when you display a digital artefact, and your colleagues tell you that they don't understand it, don't immediately throw it out. It's quite possible that it will be worth keeping. You might come across another computing lead who will be able to find a use for it, either in another school or on a social media group. If it is certainly beyond use, this can be a great way to make some extra money for the department: some schools have sold or traded old kit for vouchers or more up-to-date equipment.

There might be other more pressing matters within your subject or school, and thinking about resources or planning might seem a luxury, especially if you are being tasked with some rapid intervention in your computing curriculum. The school might be in an 'Ofsted window'. The change in the Ofsted inspection framework rightly puts curriculum coherence and quality of teaching at the forefront of the inspectorate; however, this has led to leaders anxiously ensuring that the necessary ducks are in a row, even for developing subjects. Where you are in this cycle is important when it comes to considering where to start and where to go next. However, sometimes you will have this dictated to and, sadly, that can come in the form of a very firm, 'Not now'; or 'It's not part of the school development plan this year'. As always, don't panic: reflect and focus your energy on simple small wins.

CHAPTER 2
WHO DO WE THINK WE ARE?

We have started earnestly. You may know us, or you may be asking, 'Who do these two think they are anyway?' Allow us to divulge.

Given the wealth of literature on computer science and so many other matters that make life busy, we are grateful that you have taken the time to get to this point. It is only fair then that we offer a little more information on our background. Our collective knowledge and expertise in computing, plus our experience leading the subject, has been tested on numerous grounds. We also want to refer to the word of choice previously – expertise. Neither of us profess to be experts, it's not in our nature. However, we do profess to have a particular expertise within the discipline of computing. We know that may be quite pedantic, yet, we think it's an important distinction to make none the less.

Allen – @TsuiAllen

When Karl offered me the opportunity to collaborate with him on this book, it was an absolute no-brainer. I first 'met' Karl in the year that I am sure many of us would rather forget (2020), given the adverse repercussions that so many of us see in the children that we are currently teaching and will be working with for many years to come. But out of that adversity, there is much to celebrate too. The progress that was made with the way so many people embraced technologies to maintain social connections while social distancing was outstanding. Many are quoted as suggesting that global efforts saw technological advancement transform in months rather than years.

Just scrolling through my Twitter timeline, it was Karl's presentation as part of the Computing at School #CASVirtual20 series of live webinars at the end of June 2020 where I thought, 'Wow! This is somebody I would love to work alongside.'

I had been offered the role to lead computing just over a month before. My very first interaction with Karl occurred because my senior colleagues had agreed in that first week of lockdown in March 2020 that I should work from home until the social distancing measures were able to be relaxed. With no need to commute, I used social media to remain connected to those beyond my own household. I found myself steadily building up a following on Twitter with my irreverent frivolity, greeting the day in the #teacher5oclockclub where Karl's daughter made a guest appearance at the end of May 2020. This book is therefore very much a product of Twitter and that year.

I must confess that I am not a pure pedigree computer scientist. In fact, I didn't do at all well in school, and my achievements are due to the kindness of others in providing extra opportunities. What I do have is years of experience outside teaching. When I started work, the workplace had only one standalone computer. People were so fearful of this enigmatic contraption, which could only be operated by a specialist; having proficient keyboard skills and enjoying working with technology meant I was that specialist. During my near 24-year career in the Civil Service, I was fortunate to be involved in different workplace transformation projects, from the establishment of a local area network (LAN) for the team to the digitisation of the entire organisation of 8,500 staff in over a hundred locations, with a secure wide area network (WAN).

From data processing to database design, I have been involved in much applied computing. So, my subject knowledge is good – so good in fact that one of the reasons for my bosses to offer the lead computing role to me was because, as we are a multi academy trust of ten primaries and two secondaries, I was invited by senior colleagues to support the A-level computer science students at one of the trust's secondaries during the school year 2020–21. So, I teach from early years to pre-university.

In terms of my teaching background, I had originally wanted to teach secondary computing but the joy of enabling young learners to flourish and seeing their knowledge grow exponentially made this the teaching path I wanted to pursue. To be able to combine my professional passion for working in the primary school sector with my subject knowledge and ability to teach the very highest levels of secondary school means that since 2020, I have been living the dream. Because the school where I am subject leader in computing is a three-form entry school, since 2016 the senior leadership team (SLT) had organised computer science teaching by appointing a specialist teacher as part of the school's planning, preparation and assessment (PPA) cover. I am therefore teaching all classes across the whole school, from Nursery (aged 3) to those aged 11 (Year 6). I had wanted to be subject lead for computing when I joined the school in 2015 but didn't achieve this immediately. I remained undeterred and continued to sit on the periphery, supporting the subject lead for computing with co-hosting or facilitating after-school computer club activities, as well as becoming involved in securing 'Academic Enrichment' opportunities which were digitally centred and STEM-centric.

Having been a class teacher since I qualified in 2012 means that as a specialist subject lead, I'm always mindful of the class teacher's perspective. I make sure that I let my colleagues know what I have been teaching and what their classes have been learning, to model how I expect the children to be able to talk to their teachers and families after my lessons. I expect all learners to leave my lessons being able to describe to any adult what they have learned, why they've learned what they did and how to apply their learning.

I could be one of those teachers who doesn't share anything from their professional practice. But I don't like that attitude, since I think that's actually quite selfish. Anyway, I'm not here to criticise how others view their roles as teachers. Somebody once described me as an 'open source' kind of individual. Being open source and freely sharing everything about my teaching practice means that I am viewed as completely transparent and accountable. Advocating for a subject that I have had a personal passion for since 1982 means that I am eager to help and support others reach the professional point that I have achieved. Sharing the teaching material I write and learning resources I create is a way of keeping myself accountable too, as others can provide feedback and scrutinise my efforts. Technology has also enabled each and every one of us to simply share what we create within a couple of clicks.

So that's me. What about you Karl? Why did you have this idea for this book?

Karl – @MRMICT

Echoing the statements above, I would also like to thank you for choosing this book. There is a growing number of books for teachers, leaders and subject specialists, and it really matters that you have chosen us as your humble guides on this journey. In a nutshell, every book I found about computing was either a collection of lessons, aimed at secondary schools, or was already out of date. I wanted to offer a true leadership guide, like a navigational companion on each step of your journey. This would be a useful and reflective tool to help me digest my leadership journey and synthesise my sense of purpose, my 'why', as a continuing curriculum and middle school leader. I couldn't think of anyone I would want to work on it with me other than Allen. I feel our paths converged nicely on our leadership journey, and we continually challenge and inspire each other. However, I wanted to offer something light and easy to digest, and a book that didn't need a lofty appendix to decode the text; one that could be picked up at the stage teachers needed support and put down until required again. Like Batman and Robin, the book can be your red telephone.

I have learned an incredible amount from Allen, and one of the greatest things I have learned is to take advantage of absolutely every opportunity that comes your way. I invited Allen to be a part of this project because we were both taking on the responsibilities of computing leads at the same time. We have both worked within CAS (Computing at School) and NCCE (National Centre for Computing Education), and we offered mutual advice to each other and to others on X (formerly known as Twitter). What made this even more beneficial is that with my work across the local authority in Newcastle-upon-Tyne and Allen's work across his trust in London, particularly in secondary, it all made perfect sense. We share a similar pedagogical approach, however, and perhaps the most important connection is that we are both incredibly passionate about computing and the benefit that it can provide as a school subject.

Like Allen, I was never a 'computer scientist'. However, I have always loved the possibilities offered by technology to really bring learning to life. I was always stretching the boundaries of my own technology at home in Belfast when I was younger, by making stop frame animations with my very basic Cannon camcorder, usually using my collection of eclectic action figures to act out scenes I learned in Irish history. This led to my journey as a film production student. My dream was to become the next Steven Spielberg or George Lucas, but after university it was clear that unless a move to London was on the cards (it wasn't), I wasn't going to become the next big thing in film. After university, I bounced from one job to the next, not sure what was to be 'my thing'. However, watching my incredible wife teach each week truly inspired me. I had always had secret ambition to be a teacher; my earliest career thought was to become a history teacher. However, it was my wife who encouraged me to become a primary school teacher. Sadly, I hadn't gained maths GCSE, so I had to work to achieve this. As luck would have it, I was offered the opportunity to volunteer in the school that my wife taught.

While volunteering weekly alongside enrolling in a teaching assistants' qualification, I tried to absorb as much as I could in preparation for what

I hoped would be my foray into teaching a year later. I was effectively working six days a week, as my full-time employers at the time would only allow me to volunteer on one of my days off, as opposed to dropping a day. Fast-forward a little, and an interesting job opportunity came up that I couldn't refuse. The role was a learning and equalities mentor, and as part of the job description I would create films, animation and other forms of media with small groups of disengaged children to encourage them to become more involved with what they were learning. It was an opportunity to turn abstract societies such as the ancient Egyptians and the Romans into tangible works of which the children could be proud.

I absolutely loved this job. The following September, the new national curriculum was launched to much fanfare and excitement, and words such as algorithms, selection, variables and logical reasoning were thrown into the primary school curriculum. I was always quite jealous of the computing lead, and I remember wondering whether I, as a non-teaching member of staff, would be able to lead computing if he were to leave. The answer was no.

I have always had one eye on computing as a subject. During my PGCE year I had witnessed a varying quality of computing education, ranging from incompetently passive to exceptionally brilliant. Our university lectures tended to focus purely on the information communication technology (ICT) elements of computing, as opposed to the part that I think my colleagues would now have considered to be the most challenging.

When I qualified, I was very lucky to have been involved in computing. Our assistant head was computing lead, and computer science was not an area in which he felt confident. To me it felt like second nature, and I was obviously glad to help. I was hungry to make the subject the best it could be, and although I certainly made a few mistakes along the way, it felt like computing confidence across school was growing.

As a subject lead I believe that computing is a great subject to test your ability to: disseminate information to others; clearly condense and structure progression in a 'difficult' subject; and assess and identify areas for improvement. The computing lead also becomes a de facto tech support throughout school, which has a positive as well as a negative side. One positive is the ego boost that you get when making flicking a switch seem like a complicated procedure.

I became a CAS community leader and have worked with the Newcastle Computing Hub as a course facilitator. I am proud to be the first primary school teacher in England to receive the NCCE's Primary Certificate. A highlight of my computing leadership was helping our school achieve the primary computing Quality Mark, which was a testament to the hard work of the staff and children. I am incredibly pleased with this achievement, especially since I had to push through the challenges of teaching new concepts and supporting staff to understand computing 'unplugged'. I have since become a Barefoot Computing ambassador (see Chapter 3 for more information on this computing website). I have created resources for the classroom and set up my own blog site, Pedabytes.com.

Most recently, I achieved an NPQSL, and I am now the curriculum task design lead and computing lead at Benton Park Primary School. I am dedicated to continuously improving my teaching practice, and hope to help others do the same through this book. All this I hope points to my knowledge, expertise and dedication to this subject.

In summary

We strongly believe in sharing knowledge and experiences, and we believe there is a vast community of computing leads out there to connect with. We hope this book will help you to connect with others and grow your skills as a computing teacher and subject leader. This book is your guide through the galaxy that is computing. Read it cover to cover? Or not? To conclude this chapter, a word about our own approach to reading resources.

Karl: I am a shameless collector of books on education and I famously had to carry two boxes of these books to my new school. However, they're not all created equally. Some I devour and read cover to cover, others I pick up and read when I need them. That's my view here. We're there when needed most.

Allen: I am a complete butterfly, flitting from idea to idea. This infuriates my family, and can infuriate colleagues too. However, my constant horizon-scanning is underpinned by a subject knowledge and pedagogical practice that I've forensically designed to fit statutory framework requirements. I believe that computing and technology should be accessible everywhere for everyone.

So please use the book as it works best for you, and do feel free to get in touch with us.

CHAPTER 3
WHAT IS COMPUTING?

Stay with us while we dig deeper, as this is not about offering lesson plans or resources but aiming to enlighten and encourage reflection. Our goal here is to help you understand the true essence of computing and its place within your school's curriculum. Ultimately, it is you, the subject lead, who will determine what is best for your students and your school setting.

To begin, let's revisit the national curriculum's definition of computing. The Primary National Curriculum Programme of Study says:

> A high-quality computing education equips pupils to use computational thinking and creativity to understand and change the world. Computing has deep links with mathematics, science, and design and technology, and provides insights into both natural and artificial systems. The core of computing is computer science, in which pupils are taught the principles of information and computation, how digital systems work, and how to put this knowledge to use through programming. Building on this knowledge and understanding, pupils are equipped to use information technology to create programs, systems and a range of content. Computing also ensures that pupils become digitally literate – able to use, and express themselves and develop their ideas through information and communication technology – at a level suitable for the future workplace and as active participants in a digital world.
>
> Source: Computing Programmes of Study: key stages 1 and 2, Department of Education, 2013.
> https://www.nationalarchives.gov.uk/doc/open-government-licence/version/3/

The curriculum is incredibly ambitious and states this immediately. We feel the need to repeat the first sentence for impact: 'A high-quality computing education equips pupils to use computational thinking and creativity to understand and change the world.'

Computing, as a subject, transcends the mere mechanics of a computer. It's not just about operating devices or memorising code syntax, and is much more nuanced. Computing is a way of thinking – a lens through which pupils can view, analyse and interact with the world. This may provoke some debate, perhaps even disagreement. However, we would like to advocate for a shift in how you approach computing leadership and subject development. Let's repeat that statement from the national curriculum: 'computational thinking and creativity to understand and change the world'. That's the heart of what you're building.

Let's pause for a moment. Think about your own digital interactions – beyond computers, consider smartphones, social media, the vast internet. Now think of the data. Most of the information available in the world today has been created within the last few years. It has been estimated that the amount of data created, consumed and stored rose from 2 zetabytes (ZB) in 2010 to 64.2 ZB in 2020 and is forecast to rise to 181 ZB by 2025.[1] Let that sink in. Each day, we are exposed to an unprecedented deluge of information, far more than our capacity to fully comprehend. And yet, we're adults, navigating this complex terrain with varying degrees of skill. Can we expect our students to simply absorb and manage all of this without guidance?

Astonishingly, only a tiny fraction of the data generated daily is actually consumed, with reports suggesting that just 2% of the information generated in 2020 carried over into 2021. The rest? It disappears into the vast digital ether. This phenomenon gives credence to our being dubbed the 'information generation'. We produce more data now than ever before, and with that comes both incredible opportunities and overwhelming challenges.

This rapid digital transformation presents an unparalleled opportunity for teachers, but it also sets a high bar. As educators, we must prepare students not only to consume data but also to understand, interpret and use it effectively: to guide them towards becoming digital citizens, who are not just passive receivers but active creators and critical thinkers.

---

[1] Statista, https://www.statista.com/statistics/871513/worldwide-data-created/

Activity time

Imagine you are scrolling through your social media platform of choice. Think about the posts, pictures, videos, articles and memes that you have engaged with, either directly or passively. Now, imagine the children in your class, who may or may not be on social media. They are engaging with a startling amount of videos, memes, games and data. Remember the opening sentence to this book, 'Computing is broad': this is what we're talking about. So, when we say that computing is not about machines and how to use them, this is what we mean. We have an audience of young people before us, standing at the edge of a door that opens into a world of incredible creative opportunities – or barriers to their own reality.

At its core, computing is about thinking. The curriculum literally states this. We are equipping children with the tools to become discerning and effective digital consumers, thinkers and strategists, and to that effect the aims of the programme of study are for children to 'change the world'. Ideally, we would want our children to become effective digital creators as opposed to consumers. The number of stories about children posting content that is inappropriate or offensive is increasing. Let's also not forget the adults, who have fallen foul of the same. This is because both lack the necessary skills. When we refer to 'skills', it's important to recognise that this is a broad and sometimes loaded term. Often, what we describe as a skill is more accurately disciplinary knowledge-specific expertise that traditionally required formal education. However, the daily use of technology has blurred these lines, allowing what was once specialised knowledge to permeate everyday life.

These are true twenty-first-century skills, which we will refer to as 'digital discernment' skills. The Covid-19 global pandemic held a mirror up to society and showed just how inadequate these skills are. Yet, they are needed for every single aspect of life, becoming essential qualities for navigating the current digital landscape. The digital world in which most children currently reside is very different to ours, and we need to consider that the world they will inhabit when they leave school will be vastly different to now. It is crucial to embed these behaviours and qualities within the 'whole' school curriculum, and not just the computing curriculum.

Allow us to demonstrate. People in your school probably already use different terms when referring to 'computing', such as those in this list (note that this is not exhaustive):

- ICT
- computing
- coding
- programming
- information technology (IT)
- computers
- iPads or laptops.

It is a fascinating exercise to ask staff what they would call the subject, as this can tell you a lot about their own experience of computing. The items in this list are all elements of what computing is, but as we have said, computing is primarily about thinking. Let's explore the terminology used by experts in the field when referring to computing. We can look first at the three strands or pillars of computing, and then to what is stated in the national curriculum.

Karl: I always hated the term 'coding', as it was never mentioned in the national curriculum. I did enjoy hearing teachers say, 'We're going to be doing computers this afternoon.' What?! You are doing what to computers? It's often a reflection of the knowledge or expertise within your staff body. It can also be a reflection of the emphasis a subject lead places on the language of the subject. Here, I feel it's important to note that the use of correct terminology is crucial, as this forms part of its disciplinary knowledge and enhances subject integrity.

Allen: Having been 'tinkering' about with computing and technology since 1982, I've seen the evolution of technology from those first home computers to the incredible power of those pocket-sized devices we now have. Before becoming a teacher, I was a desk jockey in a government department of 100 offices and 8,500 staff. I saw the transformation of the workplace from being paper-based to the installation of a thin-client secure WAN. So, teaching computing has never been such a scary prospect for me. I'm fortunate to have been supported by a team of senior colleagues who have a 'can do and want to' attitude, putting the interests of the children and students first and at the heart of everything.

> **Reflective question**
>
> It's important to consider what you are going to call the subject within your school and why. The title you choose for the subject carries significant meaning. Consider, for example, how some primary schools combine history and geography into a single subject called 'topic'. This can blur the lines between the distinct and complex disciplinary knowledge within each subject.

Professor Miles Berry (2013), one of the architects of the national curriculum, has a wealth of knowledge on computing education. His perspective on computing and its strands is both insightful and accessible. He effectively breaks computing down into three essential pillars that should help you structure and understand the subject in your school. See Figure 3.1 for the Berry's three strands: computer science, digital literacy and digital citizenship.

Computer Science	Digital Literacy	Digital Citizenship
How computers and computer systems work. How they are designed and programmed.	The purposeful use of existing programs to develop products or solutions to problems.	The skills, knowledge and understanding in order to participate fully and safely in an increasingly digital world.
Foundations ⟶	Application ⟶	Implications ⟶

▲ Figure 3.1 The three stands of computer science

Computer science: the foundations

This is the first of Miles Berry's three strands, and covers how computers and computer systems work, how they are designed and how they are programmed.

Miles Berry describes computer science as the foundation of a building. It can also be useful to think of it as the blueprint. Just as an architect meticulously designs the layout, structure and functionality of a building, computer science teaches children how to design algorithms and develop elegant solutions to problems, and provides them with the tools to establish the base of any digital product or innovation. Computer science includes the programming and coding that operate behind the scenes, equipping children to design and program applications.

It's important for children to grasp that this stage has its limitations, which we'll explore in greater detail later. However, the critical point to understand here is that design is as important, if not more so, than the final product. When you nurture thoughtful and intentional design within computer science, you're hitting the jackpot. Design incorporates both the 'why' and the 'how'; it exists in the abstract space where the real thinking happens. And to reiterate, computing is about thinking.

Let's zoom in a bit. Computer science is so broad a subject that it might overwhelm you at first. Even we were flummoxed at times in the beginning. Coding and programming are just one part of it, but as you start diving in, you may find yourself wondering: where does the thinking come in?

Computational thinking and problem-solving

Berry states that 'computational thinking and problem solving are at the heart of computer science'. While these elements are not explicitly labelled as a 'strand' within the curriculum, Berry stresses their importance in truly understanding what computing entails.

At its core, computational thinking is a structured approach to solving complex problems. It involves breaking down problems into smaller, more manageable parts, aiming to find effective solutions. Crucially, these skills extend beyond computer science and are valuable across many contexts in everyday life.

The Barefoot Framework: six core skills

Debate surrounds the exact components of computational thinking, but Barefoot Computing – a subject support initiative for primary teachers – tackled this challenge head-on. After extensive research and collaboration with experts and educators, they identified six key computational thinking skills: decomposition, pattern recognition, abstraction, algorithmic thinking, evaluation and logic (see https://www.barefootcomputing.org/resources/computational-thinking-poster).

These six skills, often referred to as the 'building blocks 'of computational thinking, offer teachers a practical framework for embedding these concepts into the classroom. Barefoot emphasises that while debate about the elements of computational thinking continues, their identified skills provide a robust foundation for primary school teachers and children, and prepare children for real-world problem-solving, not only in computing but in any field.

Additionally, Barefoot has been instrumental in providing resources and training to support teachers in integrating these skills into their curricula. Having experienced Barefoot's training from both perspectives as both participants and facilitators, we can confidently say that their approach makes the complexities of computational thinking far more accessible to teachers.

The idea of computational thinking isn't entirely new. Back in 1980, Seymour Papert introduced the concept, although it was Jeannette Wing's later work that really pushed the notion of computational thinking as an essential skill for every child. Her vision, alongside initiatives such as Barefoot Computing, has firmly embedded computational thinking as a fundamental twenty-first-century skill.

While all six of the skills identified by Barefoot are vital, we've chosen to focus on four skills in Table 3.1, to keep the content digestible and manageable: decomposition, pattern recognition, abstraction and algorithmic thinking.

▼ Table 3.1 Exploring Barefoot's computational thinking skills

Key computational thinking skill	Explanation of the skill
Decomposition	This involves breaking down complex problems or tasks into smaller, more manageable parts. By analysing each part separately, it becomes easier to understand and solve the problem step by step.
	Think of decomposition like a cross-sectional diagram or exploded view, where you break an object into its individual components to understand the whole. A simpler example could be something as routine as getting ready in the morning and breaking the task into steps: brushing your teeth, getting dressed, etc. This is decomposition in action.

Key computational thinking skill	Explanation of the skill
Pattern recognition	This involves identifying similarities, trends or recurring structures in data. It helps children to simplify complex information by spotting connections, which makes problem-solving more efficient. For example, recognising spelling patterns in language or identifying mathematical sequences can help children streamline their work. In computer science, recognising patterns allows students to apply known solutions to new problems, reducing the need to start from scratch every time. It's a crucial skill in both computing and real-world applications, enabling efficiency and better decision-making.
Abstraction	This is about simplifying a complex problem by focusing only on the most important details, while ignoring less relevant specifics. An excellent example of abstraction is navigating a subway map. You don't need to know all the intricacies of the entire system, just the route that gets you to your destination. Similarly, think of a secondary school timetable. For a new student, the sheer amount of information can be overwhelming, but abstraction helps by focusing only on what's necessary for getting to the next class. Abstraction is a skill that helps make sense of complex systems, whether in computer science or everyday life.
Algorithmic thinking	This is at the core of computational problem-solving. Algorithmic thinking is the process of designing step-by-step procedures, or algorithms, to solve a problem. Algorithms provide clear, unambiguous instructions that lead to a desired outcome. Algorithms are everywhere around us, from simple maths problems to everyday tasks such as getting dressed or cooking a meal. They are the rules we follow to achieve consistent, repeatable results.

These foundational skills form the backbone of computational thinking. They are not only essential in computer science but also serve as key problem-solving strategies across other domains. By embedding these competencies into your teaching, you'll be helping your students build a toolkit that will serve them well in any context.

Information technology

IT is often mistakenly viewed as the 'boring' part of computing. In reality, it's a vital aspect that involves the use of computers and digital tools to manage, create and share information. IT is about empowering children to become digital creators, and this is a vast area with significant opportunities for exploration.

One key aspect of IT is using existing programs to develop creative and practical solutions to problems. If we want children to thrive as digital creators in a world of constant digital consumption, it is essential to offer them a clear vision of how to use technology purposefully.

In the modern UK classroom, IT plays a pivotal role in integrating computing into daily learning. It provides the context for understanding how computers impact various sectors and how digital tools can be used to create digital artefacts such as presentations, spreadsheets and videos.

We focus on two key content areas:

- digital artefacts
- computing contexts.

These areas are embedded in computing programmes of study, either explicitly (as with digital artefacts) or implicitly (through computing contexts).

Digital artefacts

Sticking with our building analogy, think of this stage as asking 'what's the purpose of the building?' You've created the app or program; now, how will you use it?

Digital artefacts are digital objects created by people, such as text, images, videos and sounds. For pupils, developing the skills to use applications confidently for creating digital artefacts is essential. This includes learning:

- Spreadsheets: using formulae, and sorting and filtering data.

- Design principles: employing concepts such as the 'rule of thirds' for visual media.

In a strong IT-based curriculum, pupils can produce high-quality digital artefacts and evaluate their trustworthiness, usability and design integrity. Importantly, learners will need plenty of time and repetition to develop these skills and become proficient across a variety of media and contexts.

Computing contexts

Computing contexts offer pupils a broader understanding of how computing is applied in real-world scenarios. This is empowering, as it reveals the transformative effects of technology on society. Pupils explore everything from historical milestones, such as the development of the Colossus computer, to contemporary technologies such as the internet, and emerging fields such as data science and artificial intelligence.

By revisiting computing contexts over time, pupils can deepen their understanding of how technology impacts their world. For example, digital mapping lessons might start with basic applications in primary school, then evolve to cover more advanced technology and associated ethical considerations as learners move into secondary education.

A well-rounded computing curriculum incorporates both declarative knowledge (knowing what to do) and procedural knowledge (knowing how to do it). This balance ensures that pupils not only gain practical skills for creating digital artefacts but also develop a more nuanced understanding of how technology shapes – and is shaped by – society.

In short, high-quality IT education equips students with the knowledge and skills they need to become both competent digital creators and informed digital citizens.

Digital literacy and online safety

Online safety has evolved from being an afterthought to becoming a fundamental component of any app or program designed for children. Berry emphasises the concept of 'implications' when discussing online safety in relation to computing products. Just as a blueprint for a building serves as both a design and a consideration of its impact on inhabitants, the development of digital tools must also take into account the potential consequences for young users. 'Implications' refer to the skills, knowledge, understanding and experience necessary for children to participate fully and safely in an increasingly digital world.

Consider the apps that children engage with daily. How they interact with these tools and the impact of that interaction on their lives is profound. The consequences of negative engagement with digital products can be significant, reinforcing the idea that online safety is perhaps the most crucial aspect of the curriculum.

It is essential to weave online safety into the curriculum with integrity. Doing so equips children with the necessary skills, knowledge and understanding to navigate today's digital landscape safely, while also ensuring that staff are aligned in their approach. This ties back to the building metaphor: a well-designed computer science curriculum can provide a safe environment for its occupants (in this case, ICT). Within this framework, online safety can be viewed as the 'rules of engagement' for this environment. Just as there are restrictions in a multi-floor apartment – such as no smoking or pets for safety reasons – online safety education empowers children to confidently navigate the digital world while minimising risks.

While the core principles of online safety remain constant, the digital landscape is continually changing. The recent rise in concerns about online misinformation, disinformation and malformation underscores the need for a curriculum that adapts to emerging threats. As we develop our curricula, it's essential to recognise that online safety policy can never be truly finalised; it must act as a living document that reflects the ethos and mission of the school and requires frequent updates.

In the UK, the DfE acknowledges this dynamic landscape, updating the Keeping Children Safe in Education (KCSIE) (2024) guidance annually to provide schools with the latest information on safeguarding children, particularly regarding online threats. Schools and subject leaders must stay informed about these updates and integrate them into their online safety curriculum.

Several resources can help schools stay current with online safety practices. Two valuable sources that we frequently use are:

- Project Evolve SWGf (https://swgfl.org.uk/services/project-evolve/).
- Common Sense Education UK (https://www.commonsense.org/education/uk/digital-citizenship).

Each aspect of online safety should be articulated from your school's perspective while ensuring clarity and relevance. Remember, the goal is to empower children to navigate the digital world confidently and responsibly.

Our bite-size approach to online safety has been intentional here, and we will be returning to this subject in more detail later. The purpose here is to offer more context from our perspective, which naturally forms our experience and opinions. However, each strand has its own specific purpose and voice, which you need to approach from the ethos of your own school.

Computer science

We can assure you with a degree of absolute certainty that this aspect of the computing curriculum will be the area on which you focus most of your CPD and attention. Some of you may, like us, have a degree of experience or interest in this area, which will be helpful. However, most of you won't, but that's fine too, because you still have the potential to become great subject leaders in computing.

As we delve a little deeper into each strand to assist you in developing its purpose, execution and assessment for your own curriculum, it is important to stress the value in knowing and appreciating the subject. We understand why you might want to buy or bring in outside development, but you should most definitely begin to think about the specific 'quality' that computing has for you. This quality is beyond whether you like or dislike the subject, and whether you have any motivation to improve your skills beyond having to do so for performance management purposes. So think again, what does computing mean to you? And most importantly, what does computing mean to your school community?

Computer science is complex, but it needn't be. You might call it coding, you might call it programming, but we feel it's incredibly important to use the term from both the curriculum and the industry itself. This is where you can begin to enshrine disciplinary knowledge and academic subject integrity. Using the correct term from the academic field will be important when Ofsted and other education leaders ask how you are demonstrating and encouraging children to 'behave like a...' or 'think like a...'. By using specific terms, you can help to develop children's subject-specific knowledge.

Figure 3.2 illustrates the place of coding within programming in computer science.

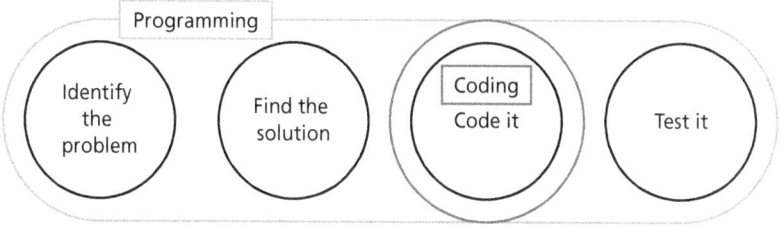

▲ Figure 3.2 Coding in computer science

In the interest of clarity, we should explain a little more. While children may be seen 'writing code' in lessons, the broader focus is on teaching them to 'program' – a concept that extends beyond just inputting code. Coding, in this context, refers to the act of adding blocks or lines of code to a program, whereas programming encompasses the wider problem-solving, design and logic processes. The diagram below is designed to show that children's learning in computing is a journey that goes beyond coding alone.

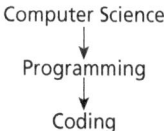

▲ Figure 3.3 The progress of children's learning in computer science

The above diagram is useful to share with staff. Having a shared language for each subject is important, and computing often needs translating, so it is always best to set out the stall and terminology from the outset. Figure 3.3 illustrates in a degree of simplicity how computer scientists work to identify a problem or solution: first, they begin the programming process and then they start to code it. This can happen repeatedly, which is why we end up with OS 16.3.4 etc.

Computer science is creative, and it is also curious. The brilliance here is that there is no single way to do things. It is indeed a science, as the science is in the thinking. Often, we are asked or even challenged to explain why children need to learn to code, given the viral-like emergence of AI (artificial intelligence). Again, this shows a clear misunderstanding of why children should learn to code. AI is an incredible advancement, but also frightening. However, it is only as successful as both the information it is fed and the small group of people feeding it. One of the many reasons why children need to understand the importance and significance of computer science is that, traditionally, more marginalised groups have historically been kept out. It is important that every child sees themselves in their future. One way to guarantee that is to ensure that they are part of building that future. However, the practical reason to ensure children understand these foundations is because there will still need to be humans. A human will always think differently and sometimes less logically, but more elegantly: this is true computational thinking.

A firm foundation in computer science ensures that children have a clear understanding of key transferable skills and concepts. For example, computer science offers opportunities to think critically and work collaboratively. In the World Economic Forum (WEF)'s (2023) Future of Jobs Report, key emerging sectors for future employment include the transition from fossil fuels to green energy and roles related to AI, specifically generative AI. The report emphasises that the shift to greener energy systems and the adoption of AI technologies are driving significant changes in the workforce. The WEF identified analytical and creative thinking as top areas for upskilling initiatives, alongside AI and big data, which are expected to see a substantial increase in demand across industries such as financial services, electronics and entertainment (WEF, 2023). Both green energy and AI dominate the media headlines. When the national curriculum was written, I have no doubt that a small group of experts predicted this and attempted to include it; however, so much has changed since the inception of the national curriculum. Thus, we need to ensure that the children of tomorrow are set up to lay the foundations of the technology of the future and that which meets the demands of the future.

Karl: From my experience, the most important thing to note is that computer science an area in which the subject lead needs to support teachers to feel more confident. Whatever you do, don't overcomplicate it. If I had a pound for every time I have been asked how to support or sequence lessons! If you are under-confident, consider delegating this task to another, more knowledgeable person. Most recently, I had to spend approximately 30 minutes teaching my year group colleague how to use Scratch before we taught it, and this isn't an effective way to teach or support. However, as I have said, any project or lesson sequence that is designed needs to be simplified so as not to overwhelm your colleagues and pupils. It is much easier to build on strong foundations than to rush to build incredibly complex projects. For example, when teaching Year 3, I always encourage staff to teach the children to program basic sequences, like a character walking across the screen. It is a sequence, it is simple, and it is far more effective to build from here than anywhere more complex.

Allen: Absolutely this, Karl. Keeping IT simple is key. From my experience of both supporting A-Level computer science students who have gone on to study the subject at university, and when I was building databases and installing hardware in the last century, computer science is essentially about building up a body of knowledge and understanding about the technology, then applying what can be achieved in a purposeful, practical way. The history of computing shows us that technology was developed as a means of improving communication and mechanising or automating physical tasks. Home computing in the 1980s took technology into the realms of entertainment through gaming. Military and academic interests converged to create early online learning platforms. Computer science can be understood as being able to apply thinking in a way that technology understands.

In essence this is the origin of our rationale for thinking deeply about the computer science strand within your curriculum. In turn we want you to be challenged to think. We will advise in a later chapter how you might 'build' this curriculum, but it is vital that you consider the past, present and future of computer science. We began to develop our curricula almost in tandem; we had regularly exchanges on social media, and often challenged each other to think about what the curriculum would mean to us, our school and its wider community.

Information communication technology

We will wager again that most teachers have some degree of experience in ICT. It is a comfortable area for most teachers because there is a degree of certainty in it, that is until the next big software development. However, that doesn't mean you won't hear teachers saying 'I just about know how to use the word processing software to create a document'.

ICT is where children are learning to use devices and systems. Teachers rightly consider this area of the computing curriculum to be creative. In a world that is literally saturated with information, it is incredibly important for children to be able to engage with it. However, we believe children should be creators, not only consumers. As we have stated earlier, the sheer volume of information pouring out of the internet is sobering. Our children can and are consuming dangerous amounts of potentially harmful data. KCSIE clearly states that schools should ensure children are safeguarded from potentially harmful content online, emphasising the increasing risks of exposure to inappropriate and dangerous material. This aligns with the Prevent Duty (HM Government, 2015), which highlights the responsibility of schools to protect children from being drawn into terrorism, including exposure to extremist ideologies. Together, these frameworks underscore the necessity of educating children not just to consume but also to create content responsibly and safely.

We want to digress a little and allude to our curriculum cousins and subject leads in English. The English programme of study's primary purpose is to equip children with the necessary language skills to communicate effectively, both verbally and in writing. By mastering these skills, pupils can express their ideas and emotions, engage with others and understand the world around them. Ultimately, the goal is to prepare children to participate fully in society, with the language skills necessary for effective communication and critical thinking.

Similarly, digital literacy requires pupils to use digital tools and platforms to communicate ideas, share information and collaborate with others in a digital environment. It also enables pupils to access, create and share digital content that reflects and influences culture, ideas and knowledge. Traditional literacy prepares children to be active and informed members of society by ensuring they can engage with the written and spoken word; DL extends this into the digital realm, empowering children to navigate and contribute to their increasingly digital life.

There are probably children in your classes or school who are adamant that they are going to become the next YouTube sensation. What's more, there is absolutely no reason why they cannot. In the same way we teach children to engage with classical texts and write in their 'style', we need to ensure that children can create quality content that is as engaging as any English work we ask them to complete.

Almost every job application requests proficiency in the use of ICT. It is a prerequisite to obtaining future employment. However, we have taught children with significantly better digital literacy skills than us. Often, 'digital literacy' is also used to describe online safety. However, for us digital literacy extends learners' traditional literacy beyond the physical and into the digital world. Being able to read and write in a world where that content is online, or part of a complex network is important. However, being able to read, create and share content that resonates with students personally is incredibly significant.

In the primary school classroom, fostering confidence in digital literacy is like giving young minds a set of digital building blocks. When children feel comfortable exploring these tools, they can transform from passive consumers of content into active creators. A carefully crafted curriculum could allow a child to experiment with a drawing program or app. With this newfound confidence, they could express themselves visually, creating stories or animations. This supports creativity and further deepens the problem-solving skills developed in computer science. It is, quite simply, the application of the foundations you will also be teaching.

As these children move through school, digital literacy allows them to confidently navigate the ever-evolving digital landscape. They will slowly evolve into the future content creators you hope for – the ones who can design engaging presentations or films, craft informative or exciting websites, or even develop interactive games. Being digitally literate empowers them to do more than consume, and to actively participate in shaping the digital world of the future.

Karl: When I was in school, the focus of ICT was typing up an essay into a Word document. Lessons were spent reformatting WordArt to look more like the Superman font, creating a PowerPoint presentation or finding some way to use Excel. Now the possibilities are endless. With iPads, tablets and phones, more children have superior and far-reaching applications at their fingertips. Most social media platforms are aware of this. They buy small start-ups that allow users to add text, transitions and create gifs.

Allen: We believe that the best way to think about ICT is imagining children being given a new utility belt like superheroes, filled with incredible tools. Our job is to show children exactly how to use each tool so that they can become creative problem-solvers.

Online safety education – digital citizenship

Online safety education empowers students to become responsible digital citizens, capable of making informed decisions about their online behaviour. Online safety is an integral part of computing, and as a computing lead you will be expected to take it seriously. It is increasingly becoming a deeply rooted aspect of school safeguarding policy, and we will elaborate on this later.

Before we continue, there is one thing we are hoping you will NOT do as a computing lead: DO NOT post pictures (or encourage staff to post pictures) once a year asking people on social media to share it widely to see how far it can reach. It is one of the least effective tasks conceivable. At the time of the internet's inception, it may have had its merits. However, let's take stock of the digital world our children now inhabit. Children talk with relatives on FaceTime, they play games with strangers online and they search the internet daily for all manner of information. They are aware now that what they send travels far and fast. The problem now is children have little understanding of the implications once their post is out there, let alone of their behaviour online, particularly how they interact with each other.

We have both received emails from concerned parents about children saying 'unkind' things to each other over social media such as WhatsApp (for which the minimum age for registering is 13, so primary school-aged children are too young to access it). You also only need to speak to a single serving police officer to have them elaborate further. This is why we moved away from the term online safety.

We both changed our computing curriculum to reflect the changing landscape of the digital world by using the term 'digital citizenship' as opposed to online safety. The purpose of this was to emphasise the fact that children are citizens of an increasingly online and connected world. We felt that online safety seemed to emphasise the 'bad things' that other people inflict on children online. What it doesn't do is put emphasis on the harm that children can also unintentionally do.

As well as being part of the computing curriculum, online safety and digital citizenship are also linked closely with the Relationships and Sex Education (RSE) curriculum (2021) and KCSIE.

As we have repeated throughout, DON'T PANIC! This does feel a heavy responsibility, but it is also an important area for the designated safeguarding lead (DSL). This interconnectedness forms a crucial foundation for school safeguarding policy. The two key sections from RSE and KCSIE are included below.

KCSIE emphasises the importance of creating a culture of safety within schools which extends to the online world. It highlights the need for staff to be trained in identifying and responding to online abuse and cyberbullying. You might think this doesn't necessarily apply to primary, but it is becoming increasing commonplace. This should align directly with your digital citizenship teaching, to equip students with the skills to recognise and report inappropriate online behaviour. Your curriculum must also respond to and challenge concepts such as digital footprints and being bystanders in situations of online abuse.

RSE plays a vital role in safeguarding children online by addressing issues such as online consent and sexting, and supporting healthy online relationships. There are increasingly frequent stories and headlines about primary aged children 'sexting'. It is important for school staff to be vigilant but a successful and thoughtful digital citizenship education encourages open communication with trusted adults, a key aspect of preventing online harm. Digital citizenship education complements RSE by fostering critical thinking skills regarding online interactions and building positive online reputations, akin to their face-to-face relationships.

This overlap is significant for school safeguarding policy because it creates the need for a holistic approach to protecting children. By integrating these subjects, schools can empower students to navigate the digital world safely and responsibly. This collaborative approach fosters a culture of openness and reduces the risk of online harm for students. We would strongly encourage you to engage and involve parents in this issue, by offering workshops, 'how to' sessions or coffee events where you can teach them about the different apps that their children might use.

We hope that this chapter has made you think more deeply about what computing is. We are less concerned with covering technical jargon and regurgitating the entire programme of study. Our focus is on encouraging you to consider your purpose and the purpose of computing as a subject. Computing enables learners to develop what the Royal Academy of Engineering in 2014 called 'learning habits of mind' and display the characteristics shown in the piechart below.

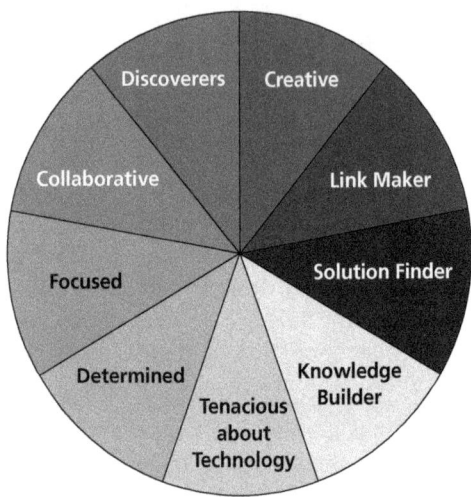

▲ Figure 3.4 The positive characteristics of the computing curriculum (Allen Tsui)

The Curriculum

When thinking about your curriculum, we believe that you need to keep in mind the national curriculum's aim of supporting learners to think creatively to 'change the world'.

In writing this book, we had several discussions about how we approached the curriculum in our own settings. Our different locations brought different requirements (Allen in London, Karl in the North East), and naturally every leader's style is different. We would encourage you to be confident in your knowledge of what is appropriate for your school and setting.

Here is how Karl developed this rationale for his curriculum.

Ambitious and inclusive

We believe children should be empowered to put themselves at the centre of their digital world. This is evident in each strand of our computing curriculum. As users of increasingly complex, data driven and ever-evolving technology, we believe our children should leave in Y6 as competent and responsible digital citizens. Our curriculum has been designed and developed to build on what has come before, using research informed teaching strategies that foster and develop a deep understanding and mastery of the computing curriculum.

Our curriculum

Our curriculum is designed to address the three main strands of the computing curriculum, helping children develop an understanding of the nature and purpose of their digital world, and how it affects their lives. Being digitally literate is widely recognised as being as valuable as traditional Primary subjects. Our ambition is that children develop their computational thinking skills to enable them to think critically about their online and digital worlds but also to be able to embed and develop key life skills, becoming effective problem solvers.

Rationale for curriculum design
We have considered clearly what skills we want our children to possess when they leave and the depth of which of which the children are doing this.

We want our children to – be ambitious critical thinkers that are actively engaged in their digital world, challenging and disrupting what they perceive.

We want our children to – participate actively and safely in their own learning, knowing the appropriate tool, whether digital or not, to solve problems effectively.

We want our children to – know how computers and their systems work; how they are designed, but also to know why and identify areas where they don't work physically and socially.

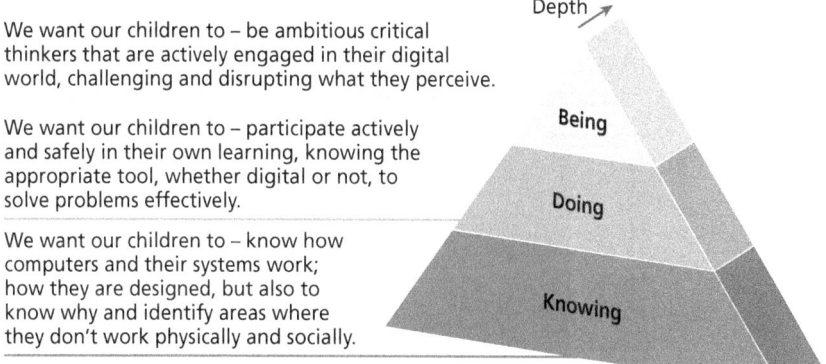

▲ Figure 3.5 Rationale for curriculum design (designed by Karl McGrath)

Karl: In the above image I was very clear about what I wanted the students of West Jesmond Primary, to be, do and know but also the intention that they do all of this to a particular depth, which was laid out in the curriculum statements.

Despite the statutory expectations of the national curriculum, individual schools can and do interpret and deliver 'the curriculum' in a myriad of ways. It might sound cliché, but one size does not fit all, although the essential minimum expectation for subject leaders must be to ensure that teaching covers those statutory expectations.

But what do those statutory expectations look like? And if by chance you have invested in this book but are working in a school or other educational context which does not have statutory obligations to follow, what framework can be used instead?

I make use of published curriculum frameworks or schemes of work for computing and computer science. Having been used in schools since 2010, the framework published in 2018 by the then DfE-funded NCCE has been exceptionally useful. To keep a track of progress and attainment, senior colleagues with strategic responsibility for the delivery of the curriculum agreed to follow this structure (see https://teachcomputing.org/blog/why-cqf).

Aside from the advantage of the whole school beginning the year with a focus on digital citizenship and ending it by focusing on informatics or data science for progression reporting purposes, this structure allows a whole term to be spent on computer science. For those responsible for leading secondary school departments, the NCCE framework includes coverage to pre-university level, and clearly signposts the amount of time that you should allocate for teaching each topic.

Because the skills for computer programming are very distinct from the learning goals for digital citizenship and data science, it is possible to choose to start or finish the school year by focusing on coding. Schools who are in partnership with other schools, whether informally or formally, might benefit from economies of scale by sharing physical computing resources if each school co-ordinates their schedules for the teaching of programming. Very expensive components can be used throughout the year by three schools, rather than each school having to invest in equipment that will only be used for a third of the school year.

CHAPTER 4
WHERE DO I START? PURPOSE

'Where do I start?' When you are taking over as subject lead, you need to think about the amount of change that is initially needed. This is where panic might set in again, although it need not. Take notice of the first thing that enters your head when you think about the change required. This is most likely a good place to start.

Your school size will often dictate the amount of change possible, and so too will the patience of your colleagues. Do contact us to share your thoughts on this. It's almost guaranteed that you will need to support staff with 'coding'. This is usually the area that we are asked to support the most. We are happy to be challenged on this though, as each school, as mentioned, is unique.

Let's rewind a little and ask yourself:

- Where do I want to start?
- Where do I need to start?
- Where does my leadership want me to start?
- Moreover, what's my purpose?

You are either a new subject lead, keen and eager to please, or you are taking on an additional or new subject from another teacher. It is always a useful exercise to consider the questions above. One key bit of advice we often refer to is to set targets that consider what is needed and what you want, but also what you don't want to do. To give yourself a sense of success, you could even include in your to-do list a task that you know will be achieved relatively quickly. While leading subjects is always a great precursor to developing curricula and a host of leadership responsibilities, no two subjects have the same needs.

Imagine that each subject was a band at a music festival that you're organising: which subjects would you put on the main stage? The DfE has already placed English and maths as the headliners, so where would computing come in your line-up? This is when you begin to develop your sense of subject integrity. What is the purpose of your subject? Why should it be on the docket? There is a list of subjects that inevitably face the cut. This is when teachers find it hard to teach; they are squeezed for time and certain subjects 'accidentally' drop off the timetable. This happens less in secondary, but it still occurs. You want to ensure your subject is in that main line-up.

When you begin to develop and structure your ideas, you are often starting halfway up the escalator without having taken the first few steps. What we mean by this is, you might have taken over a subject that needs significant work in a year that your school is awaiting an Ofsted inspection. You will need to shape your computing curriculum, and think about what it looks like in practice.

Karl: Initially, I started thinking about what I want our Year 6 children to be able to do at the beginning and also the end of the year when they leave us. However, now I frequently start in the early years. This is where the foundations of your curriculum are beginning. Although there isn't explicitly a 'computing' element of the Early Year's Foundation Stage (EYFS), I believe it comes under the expressive arts. So, I would either think about a Reception child taking each new step in their learning, or as a child leaving the school with their imaginary toolkit of digital learning. What does it contain?

Allen: It needs to contain confidence in using technology. So, I guess my priority would be digital literacy. I set some essential minimum expectations for the children I have the honour of working with – that by the time they leave primary or lower secondary (aged 11–14 years), they have become confident, discerning users of technology. That confidence comes from being able to use technology safely and securely.

Looking back at our rationale for curriculum intent in Chapter 3, it can be helpful to consider a mental image of your school's oldest students and what competencies they will be leaving your setting with. This will help you build up to this point.

As mentioned, it is equally if not more important to consider what you want your youngest children to do and how you want them to engage in this curriculum. You might face protest from early years colleagues as computing education no longer appears in the EYFS, but there are definitely elements of computing still in there, specifically computational thinking skills which are at the centre of what early years practitioners do.

You might want to start by exploring content that you can buy off the shelf as a transitionary period, and depending on where your curriculum is on its journey this is indeed an appropriate area to consider. However, we are firmly of the opinion that each school needs to 'own' its curriculum. Computing is a subject that continues to evolve, and the explosion of AI is a perfect example. Here is a concept that was barely on the radar of the most prolific computing teachers, but suddenly chatbots, disinformation and copyright are the main focus. These kinds of issue should be automatically included in a computing curriculum, and responsibility will fall on the computing lead. With off-the-shelf curricula and schemes, you are in danger of farming out your thinking to someone else.

Thinking. This is the key word here. You are the person now delegated to the role of thinking about computing. If you don't do the thinking yourself, you will never completely understand the nuts and bolts of the purpose, the 'why'. Let us give you an example.

> **Activity time**
>
> You buy a scheme of work that is fully resourced, and you want to check it out for its usefulness. This scheme of work comes with:
>
> - lesson plans
> - slides/PowerPoints
> - video guides and support
> - subject leader toolkit
> - progression graphs and documents.
>
> What is your approach here?
>
> - Do you roll it out to staff as an all-singing, all-dancing curriculum that has everything you need?
> - Do you press 'download', adapt the lesson plans and slides, and ask for feedback?
> - Do you advise other staff that it exists to help those who are less confident in their teaching, but reiterate that this is a temporary measure?

You might answer 'yes' to any of these questions, and to a degree this would be fine. Yet 'fine' is not a curriculum you want. You want your curriculum to be ambitious, but buying an off-the-shelf curriculum will not scream ambition. We are not disparaging our business colleagues who have a place in this space, but we would say that you won't understand the computing curriculum, or any curriculum for that matter, just by purchasing a scheme of work for staff to deliver.

Curricula needs to be trialled, workshopped and adapted. This is where you should start, ideally with a year group you are teaching. You can take the reins, plan and teach computing to the whole year group. If your school is larger than single-form entry, then teach in each class.

Karl: As the 'more knowledgeable other', I have historically taught computing across classrooms. This has been as team-teachers or as a more casual arrangement of 'I know more so I teach it'. Some have argued that this approach de-skills other teachers, and I agree. However, other than knowing a bit of chord progression and loving a good sing, I am not musical; by contrast, my colleague is musical, so she will teach music and I will teach computing. It's a mutual arrangement and it works. Getting to teach the same lesson to two different classes also allows me to think really hard about what needs to be improved. Or you could be like Allen.

Allen: Schemes of work in my mind are a bit like the forerunner of Artificial Intelligence. They have been hailed as the silver bullet solution but the reality of teaching is that teachers need to be confident, or have a degree of confidence, in their own subject knowledge and teaching practice. A lesson plan may have a model answer for a piece of code but if a teacher is unable to convince their students why the suggested solution is the most efficient, or offer some alternative, then all anybody is doing is simply copy typing. As teachers, we know, or at least are expected to have a working knowledge of, the capabilities of those we work with. Any scheme of work provides a useful starting point. As you say Karl, it is important to use part of what somebody else has published, have a go at teaching from those plans and see how, if any, aspects of the resource need adjusting. This process of review and adjustment is not a one-off task but an iterative cycle, especially as we teach computing and need to be mindful of technological advancements. Since 2020 for example, we have seen children as young as KS2 necessarily becoming confident with video call technology.

Karl: Once you have done a half-term of planning and teaching in your year group, you can start to see the full extent of the challenge ahead. My mistake here was then delivering a staff meeting with the all things that I had done in the previous year. It will always need to be scaled back. As an exercise, think about what you taught and how you taught it. Now think about the very basic prior knowledge needed to access it; this could be the beginnings of what your colleagues needed. You can then start to consider what is supposedly next, what you have done and plan to do, and lay solid foundations for it. This is progression, and this is building that curriculum.

Allen: Absolutely. And from my secondary experience, agree with colleagues a sequence of learning. For those leading computing in primary schools, it can be a lonely experience given that you are probably either the only individual in the entire school who is enthused about the subject or, as we've said earlier on, found yourself sitting in the chair in the musical chairs of subject leadership of a small primary school. Fortunately, since 2012, the Computing at School Community of Practice has built itself into a fantastic community of teachers who are ready, willing and able to help colleagues from other schools navigate their way into breaking down the statutory expectation statements into a high-quality sequence of learning.

What if you are already well experienced in developing a curriculum? What is the priority within this new subject? As a new computing lead you will need to familiarise yourself with the current teaching, although do not ever feel like you have to be the expert in everything. Remember that experts weren't created overnight. We have laid out our stall and explained just how the position of computing lead ended up with us.

External organisations might expect you to be an expert, but you only need expertise in one area, and that is YOUR curriculum. You need to consider what Ofsted advocates, but you will be creating a curriculum that fits your setting, and designing learning episodes to encourage deeper thinking and engagement with children's learning. The fact though that Ofsted agrees is a bonus.

Intent

First, let us apologise for using the word. You can choose any number of alternatives: purpose, aim, objective, ambition or aspiration etc. It doesn't really matter which. The problem with the word 'intent' is not the word itself, it fits the purpose (or INTENT, we couldn't help it). Ultimately 'intent' is not about what you want your curriculum to do, it is what you want the children to learn at each stage: what new knowledge will the children have that they didn't before. The reason 'intent' as a term in education has lost all meaning is because it has mutated. The number of schools that we have supported that have spent time in creating intent, implementation and impact statements, is astronomical.

Rather than spending a significant amount of time typing these documents up you need to think carefully about what knowledge your children will acquire at each stage. This then is the specific disadvantage of buying curricula off the shelf. Simply saying 'Well, it says here [xyz], then that's what the children will learn' won't be enough. This is where you need to develop YOUR curriculum.

Your curriculum

As we have mentioned, buying in is an acceptable and necessary strategy to support you and colleagues while you develop your curriculum. We cannot stress enough, the importance of pivoting and developing your own intent for a curriculum. It is difficult and it will take time, but we hope that our guidance below will help.

What is your vision?

Start by defining your own vision for the computing curriculum. What do you want your children to achieve, understand and experience through this curriculum? Consider the long-term outcomes you hope to see in your students, both academically and holistically.

Karl: For me this was as simple as aiming for the children who left my setting to be digital citizens.

Allen: 'Computing and Technology is everywhere for everyone' has been the statement of intent that my leadership of computing has been based on. The ubiquity of technology around us since I began with what Professor Danielle George described in her 2018 Royal Society Faraday Award lecture as 'thinkering' with computing has to me made digital

	literacy and media literacy as critical as reading, writing and arithmetic.
Karl:	Digital citizenship then became the cornerstone of our curriculum. This is a view Allen and I share. Your computing curriculum is your own, but it is our strong belief that it should enable children to engage positively with their wider digital world as confident and discerning digital citizens. This then allows you to build a curriculum around this vision. I was set on the idea of digital citizenship as my vision, but this came after I had led computing for a year. You must accept that you will end up pivoting again. It can and will happen.
Allen:	Indeed. Miles Berry, as one of the founders of the National Curriculum in Computing in its 2013 release, advocated three strands or pillars – Digital Literacy, Computer Science and Information Communications Technology (ICT). The risks from being exposed to inappropriate content, contact and conduct, as well as fraudulent or bogus transactions and the need to be ever vigilant from attempts to steal data or money, means that Digital Citizenship must be given greater priority or prominence, meriting its own, separate sequence of learning from Digital Literacy. As technologies advance in their capabilities to gather and harvest data from each and all of our everyday interactions, it has also become paramount to disaggregate informatics or data science from Information Communications Technology.

Alignment with national curriculum

Now you have a vision, you need to then consider whether it aligns with the requirements of the national computing curriculum. You need to consider how your curriculum supports the development of computational thinking, digital literacy and computer science concepts.

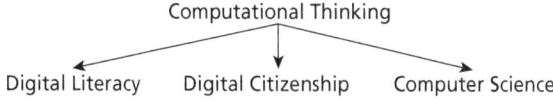

▲ Figure 4.1 The components of computational thinking in the curriculum

This is possibly one of the more difficult tasks to complete, and you might need to tweak the curriculum while you teach. Let's unpick the national curriculum statements a little, as they can be broad and difficult to interpret. Note that we will return to EYFS later, because although computing is not a specific component of the curriculum, you do need to consider its inclusion.

The computing curriculum in key stage 1 (covering Years 1 to 2) is broad and can seem a little repetitive:

- Understand what algorithms are, how they are implemented as programs on digital devices, and that programs execute by following precise and unambiguous instructions.
- Create and debug simple programs.
- Use logical reasoning to predict the behaviour of simple programs.
- Use technology purposefully to create, organise, store, manipulate and retrieve digital content.
- Recognise common uses of IT beyond school.
- Use technology safely and respectfully, keeping personal information private; identify where to go for help and support when they have concerns about content or contact on the internet or other online technologies.

We both remember looking us this and asking the same questions: What? Where? When?

'What?'

It is for you to decide the content that your curriculum will cover and how you decide to achieve that in your setting. The first three bullet points are the computer science, computational thinking and programming elements of the curriculum. We would strongly recommend a very careful concept-first approach to teaching computer science in any year group but particularly in KS1. Apart from the EYFS, this is where you lay the basis for your curriculum, and it is imperative that you ensure a strong foundation for that building, to extend the metaphor we used earlier in the book.

In the work of Shuchi Grover et al. (2019), the team explored the idea of using a mastery approach to computing: teaching unplugged computing concepts in a way that allowed the children to completely understand before they move on to any digital device.

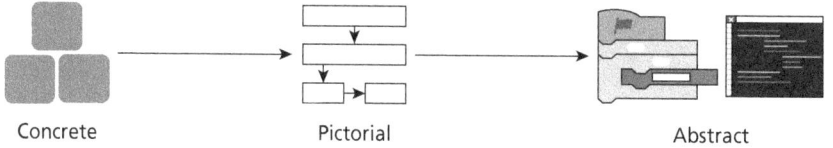

Figure 4.2 The CPA approach

Further work has been done on this by Jane Waite in her development of semantic waves; see Figure 4.3. Both images illustrate how learning progresses gradually from concrete experiences to abstract understanding. The CPA approach (Figure 4.2) shows this through a structured transition from physical objects to visual representations and finally to abstract symbols. The semantic waves model (Figure 4.3) describes how knowledge is unpacked into simpler, concrete ideas before being repacked into complex, abstract concepts. Essentially, both models emphasise a gradual shift between concrete and abstract thinking to enhance comprehension and ensure meaningful learning. The CPA model provides a structured method for this process, while semantic waves explain the cognitive transitions learners go through as they deepen their understanding.

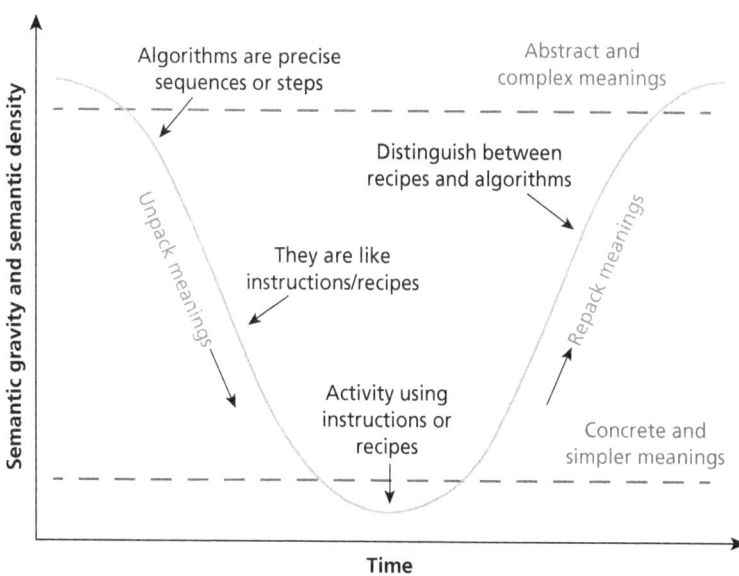

Figure 4.3 Semantic waves

Source: Raspberry Pi Foundation, derived from Curzon et al (2020), adapted from Maton, K. (2013)

In a nutshell the idea of unpacking the abstract in a way that is more accessible and more immediately connected to the childrens' lived experiences and cognitive development is not an unfamiliar one, but it is something that we often neglect to do with computing. We believe this might be down to a lack of confidence with the subject matter and an excitement to rush to the exciting bit – computers and iPads. Our message here is to take your time.

It can be daunting but there is a wealth of incredible content available that can support the development of a successful computing curriculum in KS1.

Look again at the important parts of the first three bullet points:

- Understand what algorithms are, how they are implemented as programs on digital devices, and that programs execute by following precise and unambiguous instructions.
- Create and debug SIMPLE programs.
- Use logical reasoning to predict the behaviour of simple programs.

Karl: When I am delivering training to PGCE/ITT students, I emphasise the importance of having a solid understanding of algorithms. There is so much ground to cover that there are many ways in which this can be done.

Algorithms are simple instructions or rules, and their job is to solve a problem or complete a task. Lego instructions, flatpack furniture, recipes, and directions on a map are all examples of instructions to solve a problem or get something done.

Here is an example of a set of instructions:

- Toast a slice of bread in a toaster.
- While it's hot, spread softened butter on one side.
- Enjoy your buttered toast!

This is a very simple set of instructions, and depending on the age of your children, this is a great place to start. Ask questions such as: Are these good instructions? What could make these instructions better? This could then be developed further by asking the children to write their own instructions to make toast or butter bread.

Let's have a close look at what the children would have learned by following this small step:

The children understand that an algorithm is a set of instructions. They have explored a variety of examples with you. As a class you might have explored one in detail and even debugged an example by asking specific questions. Finally, if you asked the class to create a better version of instructions, then they have also created an algorithm. These points can be summarised as:

An algorithm is ...

- Algorithms look like ...
- This algorithm could be better ...
- Here is my algorithm ...

The next step is to explore the idea that sometimes we ask computers to complete these tasks for us, and these are called programs. You can explore this using a range of apps or programs, which we can discuss a little later.

'Where?'

This is where we consider the year group and time of the year in which to place each concept or statement from the national curriculum. A few of these are dictated by the curriculum, which is important as you must not deviate from this. Following the example in the previous section, Table 4.1 shows how this could look.

Ignore the 'assessment statements' as such and focus more on the concept that should appear in each year group.

▼ Table 4.1 A KS1 curriculum focusing on computer science and computational thinking

Year 1	
Computer science	• Understands an algorithm is a set of precise instructions. • Can test a simple algorithm that they planned.
Computational thinking	• Knows that steps of an algorithm are used to solve problems that need to be achieved the same way each time.

Year 2	
Computer science	• Understands an algorithm as a program used on a range of digital devices. • Can plan and create an algorithm to achieve specific goals.
Computational thinking	• Can use Logic to plan and predict the intended outcome of an algorithm.

Table 4.1 shows clearly how the concepts and content have been progressed. In Year 1, we are embedding the understanding of an algorithm as well as how this applies to the computational thinking aspect of this concept. Next you will be able to see how this can build in Year 2 to the children understanding an algorithm as a program. It is important to introduce the digital aspect of this in Year 2 as opposed to Year 1, as it allows you to completely immerse the children in what an algorithm is before you begin to apply it to a digital platform.

As you progress further, where you should place certain aspects of the curriculum should become more apparent, and you will really start to live and breathe the content. Table 4.2 illustrates the possible progression and allocation of content in key stage 2. However, a caveat here is that this was for a particular set of schools in a particular setting and with a particular leadership. Your circumstances will be different, so our choices might not include the best place for each concept in your setting. We based our decisions on research and also trial and error.

▼ Table 4.2 A KS2 curriculum focusing on computer science and computational thinking

Year 3	
Computer science	• Read, design, write and debug a program to simulate physical systems. • Can plan and run a sequence of simple commands.
Computational thinking	• Can use evaluation to ensure their program follows a precise sequence and identify ways of improving their program.

Year 4	
Computer science	• Read, design, write and debug a program using repetition to control a simple circuit. • Can plan and run a program of simple commands incorporating repetition.
Computational thinking	• Can use decomposition to ensure their program follows a precise sequence and identify ways of improving their code.
Year 5	
Computer science	• Read, design, write and debug a program using a variable and a selection. • Can work collaboratively to plan and run a program incorporating a variable.
Computational thinking	• Can use abstraction to remove unnecessary details to actively improve their program.
Year 6	
Computer science	• Read, design and write a program using a variable to achieve a required output. • Can use different inputs (including sensors) to control a device or onscreen action
Computational thinking	• Can identify patterns in their program and use it to debug errors in their program.

Make sure that you understand why concepts should be taught at particular stages at your school. Where you place certain elements of the curriculum can often be beyond your control, but think of the needs of the school, the staff and the children: ensure that you can clearly articulate your reasoning and have the confidence to do so, remembering that it is YOUR curriculum and this is a chance for you to demonstrate leadership skills.

'When?'

This is a question that is often asked. When should we teach online safety? When is the best place to cover programming? Is it better to do it in one full block? There are many possible answers to these questions, but remember that it's YOUR curriculum, and you should base your choices on the needs of your setting.

Figure 4.4 shows how Karl allocated teaching time to cover his computing curriculum.

Karl: We had several things to consider when constructing the timetable. If you, as the subject lead, map out and timetable what you want to be taught and when, you will have a clearer picture of what is being taught and, in terms of monitoring, it gives you the ability to get to know what's being taught. One issue was that personal, social, health and economic (PSHE) education had a large crossover with the online safety (digital citizenship) content. It was much easier to allow this overlap and timetable PSHE and online safety to coincide, and the upside was that teachers could draw on a greater selection of resources when planning their online safety and PSHE lessons.

Computing LTP – Yearly overview

Year Group	Autumn 1	Autumn 2	Spring 1	Spring 2	Summer 1	Summer 2
Reception						
Year 1	DL	CS 🔙	DL	CS 🔜	DC	DC
Year 2	DL	DC	CS 🔙	DL	DC +CS 🔜	
Year 3	DC	DC	CS 🔙	DL	CS 🔜	DL
Year 4	DL	DC	DL	CS 🔙	CS 🔜	DC
Year 5	DC	CS 🔙	DL	DC	CS 🔜	DL
Year 6	DC+CS 🔙 🔜	DL	DL		DC+CS	

DC = Digital Citizenship

DL = Digital Literacy

CS = Computer Science

🔙 Unplugged – Concept First

Physical Computing – BeeBots, Edisons, Micro:bits or Crumbles

▲ Figure 4.4 Computing long-term plan (Karl McGrath – computing progression document (2021)

Another issue to consider is the landscape and layout of your school: you cannot be in several places at once, and you might find that you have timetabled computer science at a time that several teachers might be asking for your support. Often when we were entering a new teaching cycle, we would fight for some staff meeting time in order to try to bring colleagues up to speed on computing matters before their teaching began.

Cultural capital

Cultural capital refers to the knowledge, skills and cultural experiences that individuals possess and that can be leveraged for social and economic advantage. When we consider our computing curricula and the experiences our schools provide for us, this is significant. A diverse staff body brings a wider range of perspectives, experiences and approaches to problem-solving. A teacher from a different cultural background might highlight potential biases in an algorithm, whereas a teacher with a disability might identify accessibility issues or improvements. Diversity leads to more well-rounded solutions and greater innovation.

In computing, cultural capital covers a variety of aspects ranging from diverse perspectives, cultural norms, social contexts and even historical influences on technology. For us this is a key aspect to your computing offer. Depending on your educational setting, there may be very specific circumstances.

Research highlights the importance of diversity in the technology workforce and the need for inclusive practices within computing education and the industry. Developing cultural capital can help foster empathy, understanding and appreciation for diverse perspectives, leading to more inclusive and equitable computing environments. There are a number of ways you can do this but we would avoid introducing themed weeks or months. Your curriculum should reflect your school community but also the world they inhabit. Children must continually be exposed to diverse views and perspectives, and often the only place they can access them is at school. There is a wealth of stories, articles and books that you can use to encourage greater diversity within your curriculum. Questions to consider are: Do you actively encourage more girls into computing clubs or subjects? How do you achieve this? Do you ensure that you are including all stakeholders in curriculum design?

Cultural capital can contribute to a deeper understanding of the ethical and social implications of technology. Not all communities access technology in the same way, and the impact of technology on different communities and cultures is significant. There are classrooms around the world where children learn how to type using chalk board keyboards, without a computer let alone the software to run on it. Introducing children to global digital inequalities might be instrumental in slowly closing the digital divide.

Research suggests that technology designed with cultural sensitivity and awareness tends to be more accessible and effective for diverse user populations. Cultural capital can inform the design and development of technology that resonates with the cultural values and preferences of users. Developing cultural capital within computing is essential for promoting diversity, equity and inclusivity, enhancing cross-cultural collaboration and ultimately preparing our young individuals for success in the global tech landscape.

CHAPTER 5
WHAT NEXT? IMPLEMENTATION

Schools and their leaders are not short of good intentions. However, during the curriculum design and implementation stages, we tend to discover whether or not we can achieve those intentions. Implementation might be simple in theory, but in practice it can be much more difficult.

For us, the biggest difficulty in implementing a computing curriculum is managing change. Computing evolves incredibly quickly. For example, in both our tenures as computing leads we have seen the significant step up in online safety and more recently the emergence of AI. There are also practical changes: the shifts of the anticipated or dreaded software update either dramatically improves your offering at best or at worst makes it impossible and irrelevant.

Let's consider our previously discussed starting points. Your aim might be to: write a curriculum, implement it and then assess the impact. However, the reality might be: you implement a bit of a curriculum, you write some of it, you implement a little more, then you assess impact. What tends to unfold is an inevitable spiral of experimentation. If you're lucky you will run through this course quite quickly.

Karl: When I took control of our computing curriculum, some work had already gone into it the year before, mainly in the ICT or digital literacy strand of the curriculum. Yet it still needed some significant work. I found that as soon as we began to assess the impact of the curriculum that had been previously developed, it needed to be rewritten and implemented differently.

Allen: I totally agree, Karl. One of the 'Damacus moments' for me since becoming subject lead was deciding with one of my colleagues (with whom I was co-leading the teaching of computing across two primary schools) to embed the three strands/pillars described in 2012 by the demi-god of teaching computing, Miles Berry, of computer science, IT and digital literacy into teachable blocks. We arranged for Berry's three strands to be taught across the whole school at the same time: IT in the autumn term, computer science in the spring term and digital literacy in the summer term.

It is imperative that you think about this too. You may decide to do a variety of different things while identifying where you are in your curriculum journey, and this is the overlap between intent and implementation. However, we were encouraged to do the sort of SWOT analysis shown in Figure 5.1.

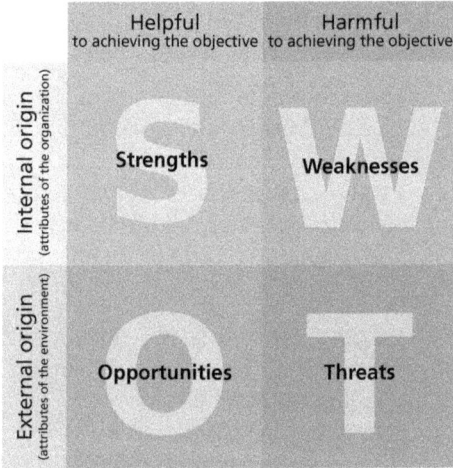

▲ Figure 5.1 A SWOT analysis

A SWOT analysis can help to identify any external and internal risks associated with your potential implementation of your curriculum. There are many potential risks to redeveloping, redesigning or 'tweaking'/adapting a curriculum: see the pie chart in Figure 5.2. Please note that the risks shown in this diagram are based on our collective experience, which includes the experience of others that we have worked with.

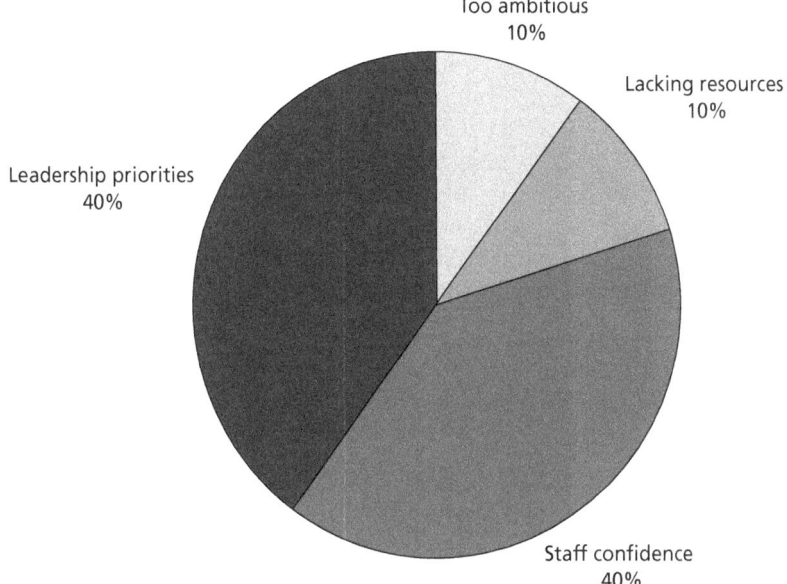

▲ Figure 5.2 External and internal risks in implementing a curriculum

This chapter will now explore these key risk factors and the potential rewards when you implement YOUR curriculum.

Being too ambitious

Let's deal with this issue straight away. We used the word 'ambitious', and we know this can be a loaded term, with Ofsted research documents often including it many times. However, there is such a thing as being too ambitious, and both of us have been guilty of this. You might include too much detail within your curriculum which is unmanageable or hard to measure, thus creating an impossible mountain to climb for you and colleagues, and the failure of the children to achieve the targets you have set for their learning. This will lead to confusion and the need to undo much of your hard work.

For example, within our curricula we have both encouraged the development of computational thinking. As discussed previously, this is a key component of the computing curriculum, yet it also refers to a fundamental set of skills that all of us possess. Computational thinking serves as a mental framework that empowers people to analyse problems and find innovative solutions. In our curriculum design, initially, we included assessment statements specifically focused on computational thinking and encouraging the staff to 'assess' the computational thinking of the class. This is a fairly impossible task: you can certainly encourage and potentially teach a computational approach, but it is incredibly difficult to decide whether one child is better at this than others. The reason for this is simple – computational thinking is how learners approach problems. You can have an opinion on an approach, but it is difficult to make a definitive assessment. So here you can see how our curriculum was becoming too ambitious.

We wanted our children to be completely immersed in computational approaches and to be encouraged to develop these 'skills'. Note that when we emphasise 'skills' here, we are referring to a part of the nuanced and at times complex disciplinary knowledge within computing.

You will encounter similar problems. It could be as simple as your curriculum statements being either too vague or too detailed, both of which can be difficult for colleagues to manage. If it is too vague, you might be being too ambitious in allowing for creativity of autonomy. If it is too detailed, this might be because you may think you have to provide support. As always, it is important to get the balance right.

You might be trying to implement a curriculum for which you don't have adequate resources. This too can be incredibly ambitious. We have lost count of the number of messages, comments or emails we have received from subject leaders struggling to implement a certain curriculum because it states the need to use resource A and they only have resource B. This then leads to supplementing a resource that doesn't fit and creates more confusion and a greater workload on staff. We explore lack of resources further in the next section of this chapter.

Finally, one of the most common ways of being too ambitious in your curriculum is the way in which you expect staff to implement it. Even with the best CPD provision, you will be expecting non-experts (perhaps including yourself) to implement a very technical subject which can often bamboozle the most talented teachers at your school. You need to ensure that your curriculum is not only accessible for each child within your school but also for each member of staff, not just teachers. Leaders will need to know and understand its importance, which we explore in a later section of this chapter. Support staff working with children during lessons also need to develop their skills to deliver your curriculum.

The word 'ambition' is used a lot, and it shouldn't just relate to your intentions for the curriculum. That forms a part of it but you also need to consider whether your curriculum is ambitious enough so that every member of your school community can succeed in learning, teaching and leading this curriculum. Does it keep everyone in mind? Does it reflect the community you serve, and does it serve the purpose you intended?

Lacking resources

Resources for the computing curriculum are important, however, not necessarily essential. We have worked with several schools in which lack of resources were a factor that needed to be overcome. More likely though is the very real possibility that you have no resources or money to invest. Computing is a subject that can require a significant number of expensive resources.

In essence, you need to ask yourself whether you have the right software and hardware to adequately support your curriculum. There are several possible solutions to this:

1. Grants and funding are available through various charitable organisations and trusts that want to invest in the education of children. However, you as the subject lead will need to consider what is specifically required when designing your curriculum.
2. Prioritise spending. If you are in dire need of a few BeeBots to excite your curriculum a little in EYFS/KS1, we would strongly urge you to invest in some. Sometimes you must beg SLT or business managers to show them and staff the possibilities.
3. Borrow kit. This is incredibly affordable and beneficial in the long term. Borrowing equipment can allow you to make great connections with other schools, and means that you don't have to store it or maintain the equipment.

Karl: In my previous school we were lucky enough to be equipped with 45 Edison robots. These little robots were incredibly versatile and relatively inexpensive. However, they were only being used by certain year groups at certain times. I desperately wanted to loan them out to other primary schools. The problem I had was time and transportation. However, I was one lead in one school, and I know there will be others willing.

Allen: Same! Being part of a family of schools – whether in a very formalised structure or just an informal cluster of subject leaders – and the power of social media have enabled so many opportunities to share hardware and resources. In 2023, I was able to run workshops for schools for BBC micro:bit through collaborations. There is a vast network of people who are willing and able to support schools in teaching 'physical computing' to incredibly high, world-class standards.

4 Go 'unplugged' and teach the concept without the device. We would argue that virtually every aspect of the computing curriculum can be taught unplugged. Computer science is about being presented with problems and finding solutions. With a whiteboard, a set of instructions and an afternoon to train other teachers, we could progress this from EYFS to Year 6 in no time. Computing might not be your subject or comfort zone, but teachers are incredible at TEACHING and computing is still a relatively new field to teach. If we compare this with our brothers and sisters in the mathematics field, then we have only had times-table practice games and digital Numicon for a short time. Before that it was block, limited cards or paper. Additionally, barefootcomputing.org have an incredible library of unplugged resources to choose from.

Staff confidence

If you refer to the pie chart in Figure 5.2, you can see that in our opinion this is one of the biggest risk factors that you need to overcome. In a primary classroom, you have different types of teachers and if you didn't know this already then please don't take offence when you realise you have been 'seen'.

LKMco (now The Centre for Education and Youth) (2015) identified four teacher types: idealists, practitioners, rationalists and moderates. Where do you think you fit? We have created our own set of teachers that you might work with and even be.

1 Professor Pixel Prowess is the go-to tech guru in the primary school, armed with a cape made of all the ethernet cables in 'that' box. Professor Prowess can troubleshoot any technological hiccup with a swift click and a magical touch. Not only can they fix smart boards and tame the wi-fi dragons, but they also sprinkle tech-savvy glitter on presentations, making them visually extravagant.

2   Your schools Code Commander leads the charge in the computing realm, armed with a keyboard and a passion for programming. They've mastered the art of teaching coding to children, turning them into mini coders. While they may not solve every tech glitch, their coding prowess is unparalleled.

3   Meet App-tastic Innovator, the tech trendsetter of the school, always ready to unveil the latest educational app that will revolutionise workload or assessment. However, their consistency resembles that of a rollercoaster ride – one day, it's augmented reality for a history lesson, the next day, a fun quizzing app for assessment. Their lessons are exciting, but predicting the next tech adventure is as challenging as predicting the weather.

4   The Digital Dilemma Dynamo is on a quest to conquer the digital world, but the journey is filled with uncertainties. They struggle when the smart board is 'having a moment' but their determination is unwavering. With a sincere smile, they admit, 'I'm still learning, but we'll figure this out together.'

5   Then there's Teacher Tech-Just-Enough, a seasoned educator with years in the classroom, having witnessed the evolution of computers from the BBC to the BBC Micro:bit. While proudly claiming to 'just about work PowerPoint', Teacher Tech-Just-Enough relies on the trusty basics. They may not delve into the intricacies of coding or advanced software, but their practical approach has weathered the tech storms.

Joking aside, we can honestly say that we are one if not a combination of these tech-savvy or sour teachers. The point here though is – how do you engage with each of these types of teacher? Our first question is who your 'fire starters' are. These are the people that can help you to light the 'little fires' of change. Charging your App-tastic Innovator to bring a digital revolution into their colleagues' practice can make a huge difference.

Leadership priorities

The final risk associated with developing your curriculum is the priorities of your SLT. Each year your headteacher and leadership team set objectives for the year ahead, and these often focus on data or areas to work on from the previous year. Strengths of subjects are important to all leaders however, and depending on how computing is performing in your school, this should be something you already know. Your subject may be one of several subjects either earmarked for specific development or just requiring a few tweaks to maintain the current standard.

You will need to ensure that your subject gets its spotlight, in terms of either time on the weekly staff meeting cycle or more revenue in the budget. Engaging SLT's focus and interest can always be tricky. We both know from experience that one year computing is the hot ticket and receives a huge focus, but the following year it could be reduced to little more than 10–15 minutes attention before the maths staff meeting or worse, just an email.

As well as fighting to get yourself on the bulging ticket of subjects, you will need to accept that this is as much as you can be given. Computing is one cog in a huge network of gears that keep the clock (school) ticking. You might be lucky that your SLT are willing and able to book regular CPD for you, but you will find that a lot of the extra work needed to keep yourself up to date will need to be generated by you. We both invested significant time in developing our understanding of computing, purely because we are passionate about it. Is it right? No, of course not. In an ideal world, every subject lead in primary will be given a TLR and the required leadership time to conduct subject monitoring. Sadly though, it isn't always possible when operating in straitened financial times, despite your SLT's wish to reward your initiative or leadership.

Leadership is about just that: leading. You must buoy yourself up with that same confidence. You are now a middle leader. Leading a subject is a huge pat on the back, whether you sought this role or have been landed with it. Having time to lead is almost always a luxury.

Karl: When I first started out as computing lead, there was no extra time for leadership. If I was lucky enough to go on a course, then the 30 minutes at the end was given to strategy. I was then given an hour each half term to focus on leadership; you can imagine how productive that was. Before securing my new role, I was lucky to be given a morning each half term, which was definitely better.

Allen: At the risk of sounding like a broken record, the power of social media has meant that being time-poor is no barrier to access to the world's biggest virtual staffroom of expertise in terms of subject knowledge and countless hours of pedagogical experience. The Computing at School Community of Practice in the UK is one such virtual network that has been running since 2012. Of the three subject associations in the UK, it is the only one where membership is free (at the time of writing). Through its various social media channels, anybody can post and connect with other members of the community. This book would not have ever happened without such connections. So let's continue the conversation beyond these pages.

Let's summarise: you have crafted a beautiful curriculum. It is responsive to your school community as well as the wider curriculum narrative. Your curriculum is not too ambitious, and you have carefully considered the potential risks. You've identified the CPD needed and who will benefit the most.

But how do you know it's working?

WAIT! Don't PANIC! It's easy to feel overwhelmed at this stage, but take a step back. Reflective practice is your best friend here. How can you evaluate the curriculum's success? The answer lies in a combination of qualitative and quantitative approaches. Here are a few questions to help you reflect:

- Are students demonstrating deeper understanding over time? Do their outputs, discussions and digital creations show growth and comprehension?
- Is there evidence of progression in both computational thinking and creativity? Can students apply their knowledge in novel situations, or are they merely recalling facts?
- How do teachers feel about the curriculum? Gathering feedback from staff can provide insight into both the ease of delivering the content and the resources required.
- What do external evaluations tell you? This might be through internal assessments, Ofsted frameworks or comparisons with local and national standards.
- Is student engagement increasing? Are students actively participating in computing lessons, exploring the subject outside of school or showing interest in future technologies?

Remember that assessing the curriculum's success is not just about outcomes on paper; it's about cultivating a thriving, confident and digitally literate student body. The evaluation process is iterative and ongoing, and you will need to make adjustments as required to ensure that the curriculum stays relevant and effective.

CHAPTER 6
HOW DO I KNOW? ASSESSMENT

Just when you thought it was all getting easy… you realise you don't even know if it's working. You are buoyed up, believing that your curriculum is brilliant and working effectively. The problem is that you don't know for sure whether or not it is. To be completely honest, there were times that we had no interest in knowing. Ignorance is bliss, as the saying goes.

Don't panic though; this is a great space to be in. At this point you can bask in your success or even better, you find there are areas that aren't working, which gives you the opportunity to stretch your leadership muscles.

Impact

You are being judged purely on whether learners acquire in-depth skills and knowledge. Moreover, you are doing this within the ever-evolving computing curriculum, and comprehensively assessing its impact is no easy feat. There might be no SATs for computing, but you need to be sure of what the children know, and this can be done through simple assessment, but you want to quality-assure your curriculum and confirm your assessment.

The Ofsted framework asserts the need for tasks that 'enable learners and young people to reach destinations aligning with their aspirations, interests, and the intent of their computing study'. Ultimately, it is the body that judges' schools and the quality of education. This doesn't mean we have to jump through hoops that they have shaped and defined. The system exists, and within it we should be confident of the environment in which we operate and the curriculum and culture we are aiming to nurture and cultivate. When you are judging the impact of your curriculum and its implementation, you need to operate in a similar way to Ofsted – be your own critical friend. Remember that Ofsted don't solely gauge impact based on academic success; they use various criteria to define success.

Summative assessment

To discover whether your curriculum is doing what it should, you need to be familiar with a range of assessment tools. Summative assessment is always useful and there are a number of tools at your disposal. The key here is evidence. The knee-jerk reaction here might be to build a folder or portfolio of documents as evidence of progress. This is not necessarily the wrong decision, and might increase your confidence. However, the important thing is being able to articulate and explain the curriculum's success alongside the solid evidence. It is your school and your curriculum. The assessment method is essentially immaterial; what is important is the 'why'. It's interesting how that word resurfaces again. Why have you or other teachers chosen this method of assessment? This is often referred to as 'monitoring', although we don't favour that term as it is too ambiguous. We would recommend using a process of 'collaborative evaluation'. This involves working alongside another colleague or the teacher/year group you want to evaluate and inviting them to enlighten you as to what is working and what is not. It's often fruitless to observe lessons unless you want to see something specific. We both know of teachers who are not confident in teaching computing. Either they are very vocal about their lack of confidence, or it is clear that computing is the subject slipping from their timetable. We are all human; if you lack confidence in or dislike a subject, you might tend to swerve away from it as often as you can. Sadly, we know that computing can be at the top of the list for many teachers.

Your job is to ensure that this is not the case. Raise the profile and increase the integrity of your subject in leading by example. This is where collaborative evaluation plays a part – you are involved, and can see the issues at first hand. A number of collaboration tools are available.

1. Socrative (www.socrative.com) is an excellent assessment tool that lets you create simple multiple-choice quizzes which provide instant feedback to the teacher. As subject lead, you could create the quizzes as you will know the important substantiative knowledge that each year group needs to be assessed on. Once the quizzes have been designed, they can be reused (there is no need to remake them each year) and you can access the data also. As part of your continuing subject monitoring, you can create target groups of children, key demographics or even target classes / year groups. You can then begin to identify the areas of support needed.

2   Google and Microsoft forms are other excellent quizzing and assessment tools, and allow you to create a set of forms that can be copied and accessed by all within your school. The positive aspects here are that they allow more information and detail to be added, and the children can write longer answers. A disadvantage however is the increased workload for staff, as not all forms can be created to provide immediate feedback, particularly with longer form answers. Overall though, these tools provide a clear opportunity to develop a strategy for support based on the data.

3   Kahoot (https://kahoot.com) is more attractive for children as it offers assessment in a stealthier approach. The interface is fun and engaging, which immediately encourages the children to compete. However, as it is bright, colourful and fast-paced, it could overstimulate some children, which could affect the reliability of the answers. Like the other tools listed above though, Kahoot provides real tangible data that you can use to assess the impact of your curriculum.

These are only a small number of summative assessment options that we have had experience with, but we believe that these are the best places to start. When choosing an assessment tool, your priority should always be how best to assess the children's disciplinary knowledge and understanding of the subject.

Digital portfolios

We have both used digital portfolios to our advantage. Using any online or offline journaling software allows the children to build us a personal or collective reflective journal on their computing learning. This can also be done using floor book in EYFS and KS1. However, another fantastic tool to assess the impact of your curriculum is *Pupil Book Study: an Evidence-Informed Guide to Help Quality Assure the Curriculum*, by Alex Bedford (2021). We believe that alongside the summative tools above, you can triangulate and quality assure this data with structured conversations with groups of the children. When done correctly it is truly enlightening to see the knowledge pour out and the connections the children can make between what has been taught. This gives you a clearer understanding of what has stuck.

Ofsted are often keen to look for direct evidence of student performance, which is where structured discussions with students recalling classroom content comes in. They will also scrutinise work, conduct observations and assess curriculum quality in students' exercise books, folders and portfolios.

Assessing other teachers

The assessment tools explored above should start to provide a clear picture of how your subject and curriculum is developing within the school. However, these methods focus mainly on student outcomes; what about the teachers?

Neither of us advocate the dreaded 'learning walk'. In our opinion it serves little purpose. You are observing a moment in a teacher's lesson, which makes up a larger sequence of lessons within a curriculum strand. It is like looking at a jigsaw with several pieces missing, and trying to decide whether or not the picture is good quality. However, there is immense value in working alongside a colleague and planning together.

Karl: I worked alongside one of our Year 2 teachers who was keen to plan a successful sequence of digital literacy lessons. The children were creating a PicCollage based on their learning in geography about local bridges. This was a computing sequence of lessons focused on the functionality of a digital presentation tool. What was brilliant was the planning of the outline discussion after each lesson and then seeing the children's output. I saw at first hand what was going on in each lesson without stepping foot inside the class to 'observe' her teach. She was undoubtedly an incredible teacher, so why would I need to observe her? Talking to the children after the lesson also demonstrated the quality of the teaching. They discussed why certain coloured backgrounds were better than others, and why the picture needed to go in a certain place. So, what was my role – a critical friend or a slightly more 'knowledgeable' other?

Allen: Make assessment part of the learning experience for the children and students. Provide 'WAGOLL' (what a good one looks like) so the children can evaluate how their work looks.

This is where we urge you to be immersed in your curriculum. You are the subject lead with the expertise, and while you might not feel confident about that, it is very important to be involved in the planning for each year group. We would 100% recommend planning out the sequence for your year groups to show what is going to go on in each of those 6 to 7 lessons.

We are not necessarily advocating creating PowerPoints for each lesson, but just being clearer and more concise about the key concepts and knowledge within each lesson. Your colleagues might surprise you with excellent tasks and outcomes, but they need a guiding hand in the input too. A happy by-product of all this is your deeper understanding of what is happening in computing lessons. When Ofsted inspection time arrives, and you are standing outside a classroom door with a team of people asking what they can expect to see when they enter the room, you will be able to articulate with confidence the elements of a typical computing lesson within your school.

Responding to assessment

Does this mean that your job is done? Absolutely not! With assessing the impact of the curriculum comes the response. How do you respond to the outcomes? There is no point in collecting vast amounts of assessment data and digital portfolios if you choose to do nothing with it.

Activity time

Look at some of your assessment data. What does it tell you? If one class isn't performing as well as other ones in the year, this could be down to several factors and you could consider the following questions:

- Does the teacher feel confident with the subject or content?
- Are the resources or tasks appropriate for the content?
- Is the teaching pitching the lesson too high for the children's ability?

If you are confident that you can support with the above, you could then look in more detail at student profiles. Perhaps there is a higher-than-average cohort of pupils with special educational needs and disabilities (SEND). Your findings might reveal that you should review the curriculum to ensure better access for all pupils, and also to boost teachers' confidence in their ability to provide this.

CHAPTER 7
WHERE CAN I LEARN MORE?

We've covered a lot in a short space of time, and yet this is only the beginning of your journey as a confident computing leader. We hope that you pick up this book as you need it, and regard us as guides and companions through the vast cosmos of computing leadership. Remember that you're not alone on your journey; the computing teaching community is vibrant, and we've met some of the most incredible educators in one of the most supportive sub-communities of education.

You've made it this far: you're confident in your curriculum, you've empowered your staff with the knowledge they need, and you know this because you have excellent assessment processes. You're already building action plans to address the next steps and changes. But what happens when you need more? Where do you turn next? Computing leadership is a dynamic space, and the community that you now belong to is thriving. There couldn't be a better time to be a computing lead. Yes, there are challenges, and yes, technology can seem like a shape-shifting beast. But these challenges are also opportunities for growth. So, when the inevitable next question or issue arises, where do you go?

Social media platforms

X (formerly Twitter)

This isn't the place to discuss the ownership and direction of X, and despite any changes, X has been an invaluable platform for us. In fact, this very book wouldn't exist without a chance encounter between us both on the platform.

Several key hashtags can signal your need for support or help you network, and we recommend the following:

- Education technology: #EdTech, #EduTech, #CompEdUK, #CASChat.
- General education chat: #EduTwitter, #EdChat, #UKEdChat.

Special mention must go to #CASChat. This weekly X chat is a gathering place for dedicated, knowledgeable computing educators. It's a brilliant space to dip in and out of, with a simple format – questions are posed, discussions follow and support is freely shared. Whether you're looking for advice, ideas or simply a place to share your own expertise, #CASChat should be a regular part of your week.

Facebook

There is an excellent group specifically for new and experienced computing leads. Over time, we've noticed a steady stream of new computing leads reaching out for support, and there's always someone willing to lend a hand. One of the best parts of the group is its large file section, which can save you hours of work. If you're about to spend five hours creating a resource, it's highly likely that someone has already done it, and they're happy for you to borrow and adapt it to fit your needs. You can join the group here:

https://www.facebook.com/groups/1043645112334322/

Instagram

This is another exciting platform, although we say this as two teachers who joined it rather late in the game. It's full of creative ideas, and there's something uniquely visual about Instagram. Whether you're looking for lesson inspiration, digital artwork to inspire your pupils or just a bit of motivation from your fellow educators, we recommend exploring this social media platform.

Non-profit organisations

Beyond social media, there are several fantastic non-profit organisations that are essential for any computing leader.

CAS

If you haven't already joined, head over to www.computingatschool.org.uk. CAS is a grassroots initiative supporting computing teachers across the UK, and we both lead a 'CAS Community of Practice'. These communities are similar to TeachMeets – regular meetings where computing educators gather to share ideas, offer support and discuss what's working (and what isn't). They're spread across the UK, so get in touch with your local branch.

Since the Covid-19 pandemic, many of these communities have moved online or adopted a blended format, which is ideal for those finding it hard to get to in-person meetings. However, the shift online can sometimes make it harder to connect on a more personal level. Nevertheless, the support and collaboration these groups offer are invaluable.

The CAS website itself is a treasure trove of resources. From CPD to subject leadership advice, it's all there – and completely free to register. The sheer volume of material can feel overwhelming at first, but their section on leading computing is particularly useful, and the website is user-friendly and easy to navigate.

NCCE

The NCCE was created in response to declining numbers of students choosing computer science at GCSE and A-level. If you haven't come across the NCCE yet, we strongly recommend checking them out. They offer bursary-funded CPD every year, so that your school can actually be reimbursed for your time spent on their courses.

In addition to CPD, the NCCE offers a full curriculum, complete with downloadable resources. Make sure however that these resources fit your school's curriculum intent, as the NCCE's curriculum tends to focus heavily on Chromebooks and PCs. Also bear in mind that this curriculum is updated regularly, so it might not be the same each time you use it. While it's tempting to simply adopt a ready-made curriculum, we urge caution. As we've discussed before, it's much more powerful to develop a curriculum that truly reflects the needs of your school and community. That said, connecting with your local NCCE primary lead can still provide useful insights and support.

One final bonus: NCCE's local computing hubs often have a fantastic selection of resources that you can borrow – completely free of charge – to enhance your curriculum. So don't hesitate to reach out and make the most of these opportunities.

CHAPTER 8
WHAT IS EMERGING?

Throughout this book, we've sprinkled references to the incredible rise of AI across the digital landscape. Given how much has changed in such a short space of time, it is not only essential but imperative that you, as a computing subject lead, understand the tidal wave of disruption heading your way. AI is already reshaping the world, and education is no exception. It's a tool with enormous potential – both exciting and, at times, unsettling. AI is currently used in education to assist with tasks such as writing, administrative duties and basic classroom support. But this is just the tip of the iceberg. AI is evolving rapidly, and the ways it can support teaching, learning and the overall educational experience are far broader than we've yet realised.

AI in the classroom

Let's start with what we already know. AI is transforming the way we approach routine tasks. From auto-marking assessments to generating lesson plans and resources, AI tools are already lightening the workload for many teachers. This allows more time for what truly matters – teaching and engaging with students. AI-driven platforms can offer personalised learning pathways for students, tailoring tasks to their individual needs, helping those who may struggle and challenging those who are excelling. Adaptive learning software is no longer just an idea for the future; it's being implemented in classrooms today.

However, while AI can assist with these practical elements, it's also important to approach it with caution. Just because it can be used, doesn't always mean it should be. As a computing lead, part of your responsibility will be to guide your colleagues through this complex terrain, balancing the opportunities AI presents with the ethical and practical considerations it raises.

Ethical considerations

As AI becomes more embedded in education, new ethical dilemmas emerge. Who owns the data that AI systems are trained on? How do we ensure that AI algorithms are not biased, particularly when making decisions that affect children's learning outcomes? These are the kinds of questions that you, as a subject lead, will need to grapple with. Understanding these issues will be vital for ensuring that AI is used responsibly and equitably in your school.

Moreover, there are questions about transparency and accountability. If an AI system makes a recommendation about a student's learning journey, who is responsible for that decision? Teachers, schools and leaders need to remain in control, using AI as a tool and not as a decision-maker. It's crucial to maintain professional judgment while integrating AI into the classroom.

AI and the wider curriculum

AI will not just change how we teach computing but will also influence how we think about the wider curriculum. As AI becomes more prevalent, students will require different skills: coding, once seen as a specialist skill, could become as essential as literacy and numeracy; computational thinking and problem-solving will become more important as students need to understand how AI works, how to harness it and how to navigate a world increasingly shaped by these technologies.

As a computing lead, you'll play a critical role in ensuring your school's curriculum remains relevant. Part of your job will be to help staff and students develop an understanding of AI, not only as a tool but also as a concept. You might need to introduce lessons on machine learning, ethics in technology, or even looking at how AI is shaping industries beyond education.

Beyond AI: what's next?

While AI is undeniably the frontrunner of emerging technologies, it is not the only development on the horizon. Other technologies are set to change the landscape of computing education in the years to come. Virtual Reality (VR) and Augmented Reality (AR), for example, are already finding their way into classrooms, offering immersive learning experiences that go beyond traditional textbooks and screens. Students are able to explore ancient civilisations or walk through the human body, all through the power of VR. These technologies are still developing, but they have the potential to revolutionise how subjects are taught and understood.

Quantum computing is a field still in its infancy but one with the potential to make current computers look like relics. While it is unlikely that quantum computing will make its way into the primary classroom soon, as a computing lead you should keep an eye on these developments to stay ahead of the curve. Who knows how education will evolve as these technologies mature?

The Internet of Things (IoT) is another growing area. Increasing numbers of everyday objects are being connected to the internet, from smart thermostats to wearable clothing. In education, IoT has the potential to create smarter, more responsive learning environments. Imagine a classroom where the lights, heating and even seating arrangements adapt to the students' needs in real time.

Cybersecurity: a growing concern

With all this emerging technology comes a growing need for robust cybersecurity. As more devices and systems become connected, the risks to personal data and school networks increase. Ensuring that both staff and students are aware of these risks, and know how to protect themselves, will become an even more critical part of your role as a computing lead. Cybersecurity isn't just a topic for techies anymore – it's something every educator and student will need to understand.

Building a digital resilience curriculum is essential. This will involve teaching not only how to avoid phishing attacks and create secure passwords but also the more nuanced aspects of cybersecurity, such as digital citizenship and understanding the moral implications of technology use. You might have a wide range of ages within your school, so your digital resilience curriculum will need to meet the needs of your community and the developmental stage of the children.

Preparing for the future

So, what does this mean for you as a computing subject lead? It means staying informed, staying curious and staying agile. The digital world is changing at an unprecedented pace, and part of your role will be to guide your school through these shifts, ensuring that students are equipped not only with the skills they need now but with the mindset to adapt to future changes.

It also means preparing your staff to feel confident in using these technologies, to understand both the opportunities and challenges they bring, and to approach them with a critical yet open mind. You are not, however, an IT expert. Nor are you a technician. You are a leader and a guide. Approach this with clarity and structure, much like the manager of a successful tech firm. Introduce new information in manageable doses: too much all at once can be overwhelming for staff and students alike.

In essence, your role as a computing lead is about far more than managing the day-to-day teaching of computing. It's about becoming a navigator for the entire school, steering through a world of emerging technologies, ethical dilemmas and new learning opportunities. You are not just preparing students for the world of today, you are preparing them for the world of tomorrow.

And remember, your success as a computing lead isn't measured by how much you know about the latest technology, but rather how effectively you empower your colleagues and students to navigate this digital landscape confidently. By fostering a culture of curiosity, resilience and digital creativity, you can equip them to be active participants in an ever-evolving world.

The key is to keep learning, keep questioning and remain flexible. You will not always have the answers, and that's fine. But by leading with a clear vision, encouraging collaboration and embracing the challenges that arise, you will not only strengthen computing in your school but inspire a generation of learners who are ready to shape the future.

Ultimately, the most important thing you can do as a computing lead is to enjoy the journey. The path will be challenging at times, but the opportunities to influence and inspire are endless. So take a deep breath, embrace your role, and remember – you've got this…and please DON'T PANIC!

REFERENCES

Berry, M. (2013). 'Computing in the National Curriculum: A guide for primary teachers'. British Computer Society.

Curzon, Paul, Waite, Jane , Maton, Karl, and Donohue, James. (2020). 'Using semantic waves to analyse the effectiveness of unplugged computing activities'. In *Proceedings of the 15th Workshop on Primary and Secondary Computing Education*. Association for Computing Machinery, New York, NY, USA, Article 18, 1–10.

Department for Education (DfE) (2013). National Curriculum in England: Computing programmes of study. Available at: www.gov.uk/government/publications/national-curriculum-in-england-computing-programmes-of-study (Accessed: 22 September 2024).

Department of Education (2013) Computing Programmes of Study: key stages 1 and 2, Available at https://assets.publishing.service.gov.uk/media/5a7c576be5274a1b00423213/PRIMARY_national_curriculum_-_Computing.pdf. (Accessed: 14 January 2025).

Department for Education (2024). Keeping Children Safe in Education: Statutory guidance for schools and colleges. Available at: www.gov.uk/government/publications/keeping-children-safe-in-education--2 (Accessed: 1 December 2024).

HM Government (2023). The Prevent Duty: Departmental advice for schools and childcare providers. Available at: https://www.gov.uk/government/publications/prevent-duty-guidance (Accessed: 24 September 2024).

Grover, S., Jackiw, N. and Lundh, P. (2019). 'Concepts before Coding: Non-programming interactives to advance learning of introductory programming concepts in middle school'. *Computer Science Education*, 29(3): 1–30.

Maton, Karl (2013) 'Making Semantic waves. A key to cumulative knowledge building'. *Linguistics and Education* 24(1) 8-22.

The Centre for Education and Youth (2015). 'Why Teach?' Available at: https://cfey.org/wp-content/uploads/2015/11/Why-Teach-Leaflet-Final-copy-for-dissemination.pdf (Accessed: 27 February 2025).

Teach Computing Blog (2020). 'Quick Read: Using semantic waves to improve explanations and learning activities in computing'. Available at: https://blog.teachcomputing.org/quick-read-6-semantic-waves/ (Accessed: 3 December 2024).

World Economic Forum (WEF) (2023) 'The Future of Jobs Report 2023'. Available at: www.weforum.org/publications/the-future-of-jobs-report-2023/ (Accessed: 22 September 2024).